W9-CII-013

thoreau's wildflowers

As the ice melts in the swamps I see the horn-
shaped buds of the skunk cabbage, green with a
bluish bloom, standing uninjured, ready to feel
the influence of the sun. The most prepared for
spring—to look at—of any plant.

thoreau's wildflowers

HENRY DAVID THOREAU

Illustrated by Barry Moser

Edited by Geoff Wisner

Yale
UNIVERSITY PRESS

New Haven and London

Published with assistance from the foundation
established in memory of James Wesley Cooper
of the Class of 1895, Yale College.

Yale University Press books may be purchased in
quantity for educational, business, or promotional use.
For information, please e-mail sales.press@yale.edu
(US office) or sales@yaleup.co.uk (UK office).

Designed by Sonia Shannon.
Set in Adobe Garamond and Zapfino types by
Tseng Information Systems, Inc.
Printed in the United States of America.

Library of Congress Control Number: 2015953455
ISBN 978-0-300-21477-2
A catalogue record for this book is available from the
British Library.

This paper meets the requirements of ANSI/NISO
Z39.48–1992 (Permanence of Paper).

10 9 8 7 6 5 4 3 2 1

Contents

Preface

FOR MANY YEARS, Thoreau's self-appointed task was to roam the woodlands, meadows, and marshes of his native Concord—observing plants, animals, the weather, and his neighbors, then recording his observations in his Journal.

Beginning in 1850, the year Thoreau turned thirty-three, his botanical observations became more systematic. He began carrying plants home in his straw hat and pressing them for later study. He dated his Journal entries more consistently, noting when certain plants flowered and referring to them by their Latin names. He read his way through all the available botanical authorities and made it his goal to learn botanical taxonomy and to know every plant that grew in Concord, even the inconspicuous grasses and sedges that professional botanists often overlooked.

As his botanical expertise grew, so did his artistic sensibilities. By 1850, his two-year sojourn at Walden Pond was behind him, and he was engaged in the task of shaping his experience into a classic work of American mythology, a task that required seven distinct manuscript revisions and was not completed until 1854, when *Walden; or, Life in the Woods* was published. Thoreau's concern with the flowering plants of Concord, which lasted the decade or so that was left to him, was aesthetic, philosophical, and spiritual as much as it was scientific.

Thoreau's Wildflowers offers a generous selection of some of Thoreau's most evocative writings on the hundreds of flowering trees and plants that he knew, loved, and closely observed. It includes only a fraction of the record he left in his Journal. Each observation is arranged by the day of the year and presented in the context of the day's weather, the presence of other plants and animals, and Thoreau's own mood and philosophical speculations.

The result is a panorama of the natural world that surrounded Thoreau, as it changed over the course of a year. More than an account of the natural history of Concord, this record is also an investigation of the spiritual significance of wildflowers for Thoreau, especially as they illustrate a central theme of his spiritual life: that of anticipation. The early buds Thoreau discovered in the winter were an implicit promise that spring and life would return. By attuning himself to the life around him, Thoreau found that he was able to anticipate not only the change of the seasons but the habits of the particular plants he sought.

In his consideration of wildflowers, Thoreau gave equal attention to the delicate blooms of herbaceous plants, trees, and grasses, including "ghostly" parasitic bloomers like Indian pipe and pinesap. He also recognized and responded to the flowerlike appearance of autumnal foliage, like the canopies of maples and scarlet oaks. For the purposes of this book, I have included passages that highlight both flowers and these flowerlike phenomena, with an emphasis on wild plants and on naturalized plants that, as Thoreau put it, have "strayed into the woods from the cultivated stock"—including his beloved wild apples. Keeping my focus on the flora of Concord as it changes through the year, I have omitted plants that Thoreau observed on his excursions to Cape Cod, Maine, New Hampshire, Vermont, and beyond.

The more than two hundred black-and-white drawings that appear in this book were created by the renowned artist and illustrator Barry Moser. They first appeared as illustrations in *Flowering Plants of Massachusetts* by Vernon Ahmadjian, published by the University of Massachusetts Press in 1979. This was the first of dozens of books that Moser has illustrated in a long and honored career. These include *The Pennyroyal Caxton Bible,* the Arion Press edition of *Moby-Dick,* and the biographies *Emerson: A Mind on Fire* and *Thoreau: A Life of the Mind* by Robert D. Richardson. By allowing his work to be reprinted here, Moser has made possible an unprecedented pairing of botanical expertise with literary and artistic excellence.

Thoreau's Wildflowers will provide pleasure and insights to naturalists, gardeners, lovers of beauty, aspiring scientists, students of American lit-

erature, and Thoreau enthusiasts. Together with Thoreau's inspired yet detailed botanical observations and Barry Moser's illustrations, it offers an
intimate portrait of "Thoreau as Botanist" by Ray Angelo, who is widely
recognized as the leading authority on the flowering plants of Concord
and on Thoreau's botanical record.

Acknowledgments

FOR THEIR HELP in the preparation of this book, I thank Gary Paul Nabhan, Marco Wilkinson, Stephen Stinehour, Kathy Crosby of the Brooklyn Botanic Garden library, and Jeffrey S. Cramer and Matthew Burne of the Thoreau Institute at Walden Woods. It has been a pleasure to work with the staff of Yale University Press, especially Jean Thomson Black, Samantha Ostrowski, and Laura Dooley.

Special thanks to Ray Angelo for allowing me to reprint his classic essay "Thoreau as Botanist" and to Barry Moser for agreeing to pair the words of Thoreau with his drawings of the flowering plants of Massachusetts. I am grateful to Cherrie Corey for an expert firsthand introduction to the plants of Great Meadows, for her helpful suggestions as the book was developing, and for her careful botanical review.

I thank Mike Frederick of the Thoreau Society for allowing me to present a preview of *Thoreau's Wildflowers* at the society's annual gathering in Concord. I am grateful for the warm welcome and offers of assistance I received from my copanelists Jym St. Pierre and Michiko Ono, and from presenters and attendees, including Mark Gallagher, Richard Higgins, Joe Moldenhauer, Nikita Pokrovsky, Audrey Raden, and Corinne Smith.

As always, many thanks to Jenn for her love and patience.

Introduction

AFTER GRADUATING FROM Harvard College in 1837, Henry David Thoreau returned to the village of Concord, where he taught school with his older brother, John. At least once a week the Thoreau brothers took the students out for a walk or a boating excursion.

On one of these walks, wrote F. B. Sanborn in his 1917 biography, Thoreau stopped, knelt down, plucked something from the ground, and asked a boy named Henry Warren if he could see it. "Drawing his microscope, Thoreau showed the boy that, thus magnified, this little thing was a perfect flower, just then in the season of its blossoming."

Thoreau's education in flowers began early, with childhood lessons in botany at Concord Academy, and continued (somewhat casually) at Harvard. "My first botany as I remember," Thoreau noted years later, "was Bigelow's plants of Boston and vicinity which I began to use about twenty years ago—looking chiefly for the popular names and the short references to the localities of plants even without any regard to the plant. I also learned the names of many—but without using any system, I forgot them soon. I was not inclined to pluck flowers—preferred to leave them where they were, liked them best there."

Thoreau's love of flowers was noticed by those around him. Louisa May Alcott, a child when Thoreau was living at Walden Pond (1845 to 1847), wrote about that time years later: "On certain days, he made long pilgrimages to find 'the sweet rhodora in the wood,' welcoming the lonely flower like a long-absent friend."

In the introduction to *Mosses from an Old Manse,* published in 1846, Nathaniel Hawthorne wrote about his friend and sometime skating companion: "The pond lily grows abundantly along the margin—that delicious flower, which, as Thoreau tells me, opens its virgin bosom to the first sunlight and perfects its being through the magic of that genial kiss. He has beheld beds of them unfolding in due succession as the sunrise stole gradually from flower to flower—a sight not to be hoped for unless when a poet adjusts his inward eye to a proper focus with the outward organ."

Around 1850, Thoreau's study of Concord's flora intensified. "I found myself again attending to plants with more method—looking out the name of each one and remembering it. I began to bring them home in my hat, a straw one with a scaffold lining to it—which I called my botany box. I never used any other. And when some whom I visited were evidently surprised at its dilapidated look as I deposited it on their front entry table, I assured them it was not so much my hat as my botany box." Thoreau pressed some flowers in the pages of *Primo Flauto,* an old music book of his father's that he carried with him.

The observation of flowers was a very deliberate activity for Thoreau. Knowing when each one first sprouted, blossomed, set seed, and died was a key element in his grand project of creating a master "Kalendar" that would track each daily change in the natural world of Concord.

"I soon found myself observing when plants first blossomed and leafed, and I followed it up early and late—far and near several years in succession—running to different sides of the town and into the neighboring towns often between twenty and thirty miles in a day. I often visited a particular plant four or five miles distant half a dozen times within a fortnight, that I might know exactly when it opened—besides attending to a great many others in different directions and some of them equally distant, at the same time. At the same time I had an eye for birds and whatever else might offer."

As early as 1851, he began compiling the first of what Bradley Dean called "many hundreds of phenological lists and charts on every conceivable seasonal phenomenon, such as the migration cycles of birds or the leafing, flowering, fruiting, and seeding of plants." From 1860 to 1862, he consolidated his seasonal observations of plants onto ledger sheets, part of a project left uncompleted with his death.

To follow in Thoreau's footsteps through the year, beginning with snowmelt in March and the first buds of the skunk cabbage, is to witness a first-rate detective at work. But few had the opportunity to witness this in person. As Ray Angelo notes in "Thoreau as Botanist," Edward Hoar, Minot Pratt, and his own sister Sophia were the only Concord residents who shared his botanical interests in any depth. None of these was a regular walking companion.

Thoreau's most frequent companion was a good friend but no botanist, the ne'er-do-well son of a prominent Boston family named Ellery Channing. Channing appears a number of times in *Thoreau's Wildflowers*, sometimes by name and sometimes as "C." According to Walter Harding, "He dabbled in poetry but succeeded in writing few (if any) memorable lines. Eccentric and cranky, he quarreled with almost everyone he knew, including his wife and children and Thoreau's mother who could not abide him. But for some unknown reason he and Thoreau hit it off well and once Channing moved to Concord in 1843, they took innumerable walks together."

By his own account, Thoreau knew at least four hundred of the local flowers. ("I reckon that about nine tenths of the flowers of the year have now blossomed," he wrote on July 26, 1853, and five days later, "I calculate that less than forty species of flowers known to me remain to blossom this year.") He could identify these flowers not only from their blossoms but from their first shoots, their dry seedpods, and their fragrance.

One of the pleasures of Thoreau's flower writing is his attention to scent: the "mild sweet vernal scent" of the willow catkins, the "rummy scent" of the wild cherry, and the pure, sweet, virginal fragrance of the water lily. He notes the barberry's "sickening buttery odor—as of an underdone butter pudding" and the odor of the carrion flower, which "smells exactly like a dead rat in the wall."

Some scents present mysteries that puzzle even a great detective. "Here on this causeway," he writes on May 16, 1852, "is the sweetest fragrance I have perceived this season, blown from the newly flooded meadows. I cannot imagine what there is to produce it." (Meadows, for Thoreau, generally meant wetlands that were flooded for part of the year.) The following year he smelled it again: "the first whiff of that ineffable fragrance from the Wheeler meadow." But it was not until 1859 that he plucked a blossom of perfoliate bellwort and thought he had the solution: "Just after plucking it I perceived what I call the *meadow* fragrance though in the woods—but

I afterward found that this flower was *peculiarly* fragrant, and its fragrance like *that,* so it was probably this which I had perceived."

In May 1856, Ralph Waldo Emerson took a walk with Thoreau to Saw-mill Brook. "He was in search of yellow violet (*pubescens*) and *menyanthes* which he waded into the water for & which he concluded, on examina-tion, had been out five days. Having found his flowers, he drew out of his breast pocket his diary & read the names of all the plants that should bloom on this day, 20 May; whereof he keeps account as a banker when his notes fall due." Remembering that pocket diary six years later, after his younger friend had died, Emerson wrote, "He honored certain plants with special regard, and, over all, the pond lily,—then, the gentian, and the *Mikania scandens,* and 'life-everlasting,' and a bass-tree which he visited every year when it bloomed, in the middle of July."

As Emerson makes plain, Thoreau was not content to walk the same routes and simply note the flowers he saw. Instead he sought out the places where sun and landscape would bring them out first. Conantum Cliff was one of these places: a sunny rock face where columbines and saxifrage grew from the chinks in the stone. In 1857 he wrote, "It takes several years' faith-ful search to learn where to look for the earliest flowers."

The word "faithful" is telling. Thoreau's life among wildflowers and other plants had a spiritual importance. He once courted controversy by speculating that a pine tree might have a soul. In the passage that gave its name to the posthumous book *Faith in a Seed,* he wrote, "Though I do not believe a plant will spring up where no seed has been, I have great faith in a seed. Convince me that you have a seed there, and I am prepared to expect wonders."

In his Journal, Thoreau often looked to flowers to reinforce his some-times faltering belief that the seasons would continue to turn and that spring and new life would come once again. In January 1853 he pulled up a crowfoot and found deep inside it the tiny white bud of a blossom to come: "There it patiently sits or slumbers, how full of faith, informed of a spring which the world has never seen, the promise and prophecy of it shaped somewhat like some Eastern temples, in which a bud-shaped dome o'ertops the whole."

Perhaps more than any of his other work, Thoreau's writings on wild-flowers bring out one of the key themes of his spiritual life: that of anticipation. As Thoreau wrote in *Walden,* "To anticipate, not the sunrise and the dawn merely, but, if possible, Nature herself!" In his 1958 book *Consciousness in Concord,* Perry Miller used this quotation as a touchstone, devoting a chapter to the theme of anticipation in Thoreau and finding it central to both *Walden* and the Journal.

Miller wrote, "The verb is 'anticipate': all *Walden* is an adroitly suspended anticipation of the climax of thawing sand and clay in the railroad cut; all the *Journal*—earnestly before the completion of *Walden,* more stridently thereafter—is a stratagem to anticipate, and so to survive, the winter. . . . If you read the *Journal* consecutively you see that every winter is a retirement to prepared positions. At last there is only one stronghold: the mind can *anticipate* spring."

Linked to the idea that faith requires anticipating the seasons to come is the notion that we find rare flowers only when we are prepared to find them—that is, when we anticipate them.

"I commonly observe," Thoreau wrote, "that I make my most interesting botanical discoveries when I [am] in a thrilled and expectant mood, perhaps wading in some remote swamp where I have just found something novel and feel more than usually remote from the town. Or some rare plant which for some reason has occupied a strangely prominent place in my thoughts—for some time—will present itself. My expectation ripens to discovery. I am prepared for strange things."

In November 1858, usually the bleakest month in Thoreau's calendar, he found himself gazing out from Conantum Cliff. The blazing colors of the maples were gone, and asters and tansy were among a handful of flowers still in bloom. But the leaves of the scarlet oaks, he noticed, still glowed here and there in the landscape. These trees, the last to lose their autumn colors, stood out like "redcoats in the forest army."

The whole forest, he realized, was "a flower garden, in which these late roses burn, alternating with green, while the so-called 'gardeners' working here and there perchance beneath with spade and water pot, see only a few little asters amid withered leaves (for the shade that lurks amid their foliage does not report itself at this distance)."

In this autumnal season when flowers seemed to have nothing more to offer, he found himself in a world where "blossoms" towered over him. "This late forest flower surpasses all that spring or summer could do. Their colors were but rare and dainty specks—which made no impression on a distant eye. Now it is an extended forest or a mountainside that bursts into bloom through or along which we may journey from day to day."

Thoreau saw the scarlet oaks because he was finally prepared to see them. "There is just as much beauty visible to us in the landscape as we are prepared to appreciate—not a grain more." This vision, once he was ready for it, was extraordinarily powerful. Botanical knowledge and spiritual insight had combined to offer him an expanded understanding of the landscape and its beauty.

"The scarlet oak must in a sense be in your eye when you go forth," he wrote. "We cannot see anything—until we are possessed with the idea of it, and then we can hardly see anything else."

"May my life be not destitute of its Indian summer," Thoreau wrote in September 1851. "A season of fine and clear mild weather in which I may prolong my hunting before the winter comes. When I may once more lie on the ground with faith as in spring—and even with more serene confidence." It was a wish that would not be granted.

Henry David Thoreau died in 1862, at the age of forty-four. His casket, placed in the vestibule of the First Parish Church in Concord, was covered with wildflowers. A wreath of andromeda was placed inside. Louisa May Alcott was among the mourners, and in a letter written afterward she wrote that early violets were blooming in the churchyard.

After Thoreau's death, the Concord shopkeeper and photographer Alfred Hosmer took up the task of compiling a great Kalendar of Concord. Hosmer first recorded the flowering times of local plants in 1878, resumed his observations a decade later in 1888, and continued them regularly until 1902.

A century later, from 2003 to 2006, Professor Richard B. Primack and then–graduate student Abraham J. Miller-Rushing repeated these observations, visiting Concord two or three days a week between March and October. They observed the first flowering dates of more than five hundred species, then compared the dates of forty-three common species that Thoreau and Hosmer had also observed. On average, they wrote in *Arnoldia,* the magazine of Harvard's Arnold Arboretum, the forty-three species were now blooming about a week earlier than they did in Thoreau's lifetime—a difference they attributed to the warming effect of urbanization and global climate change. Some species were affected more dramatically than others. The highbush blueberry (*Vaccinium corymbosum*) was flowering twenty-one days earlier than it was when Thoreau looked for it. The yellow wood-sorrel (*Oxalis stricta*) blossomed thirty-two days before the time set out for it in Thoreau's Kalendar.

At the end of his famous eulogy of Thoreau, Ralph Waldo Emerson offered the fanciful picture of his younger friend climbing steep mountains in Switzerland in search of the edelweiss flower—a notion that was metaphorically if not biographically apt. "Thoreau seemed to me living in the hope to gather this plant, which belonged to him of right. The scale on which his studies proceeded was so large as to require longevity, and we were the less prepared for his sudden disappearance. The country knows not yet, or in the least part, how great a son it has lost." Even today, as we begin to recognize the beauty and significance of the botanical record he left behind, we are taking the measure of his greatness once again.

A Note on the Text

THE EARLIEST SELECTIONS in *Thoreau's Wildflowers* are from 1850, the first year in which Thoreau made regular dated observations of the flora of Concord, though he had little botanical experience at that point. This was also around the time he began to see the Journal as a work of art in its own right, not simply a quarry from which to mine other books and essays.

The text is drawn from the fourteen-volume 1906 edition of *The Journal of Henry D. Thoreau,* edited by Bradford Torrey and Francis H. Allen. Each selection for the period between May 31, 1850, and September 3, 1854, has been checked against the Princeton University Press edition of the Journal, of which eight volumes have so far been published. Later selections have been checked against the unedited transcript of the Journal, made available online by the University of California Santa Barbara Library.

Bracketed text (mostly names of plants) has been added by Torrey and Allen or by me. Omitted text is indicated by ellipses without brackets. Penciled additions by Thoreau, rendered as footnotes in the 1906 edition, are included in parentheses. Words and phrases in italics were emphasized in the original.

The Princeton edition and unedited transcripts offer the most accurate available version of what Thoreau actually wrote, including his misspellings, sentence fragments, idiosyncratic capitalization, and haphazard punctuation. I have referred to these texts to correct misreadings, restore paragraph breaks, and change the spellings and punctuation used in the 1906 edition to something closer to Thoreau's original version.

In 1854, when *Walden* was published, and in 1906, when Thoreau's Journal appeared in full (or nearly so), authors and editors had definite ideas of what was required to make a manuscript fit for the public. Those ideas included an approach to punctuation that today seems overly fussy. In *The New Thoreau Handbook,* Michael Meyer mentions a single sentence in *Walden* that contains three hundred fifty words, forty commas, ten semicolons, and one dash. Many passages in the 1906 edition of the Journal are similarly equipped with commas, semicolons, or even a comma plus a dash. The result is a leisurely, meditative, even sleepy pace.

Thoreau's natural style, as seen in the Princeton edition and transcripts of the Journal, was very different. Like Emily Dickinson in her verse, Thoreau's favorite punctuation mark was the dash, and he used it in lieu of a comma, semicolon, or paragraph break. As in Dickinson, the dash lends his words a tense, taut, flashing quality that in the nineteenth century was called "nervous." Thoreau often uses a dash to set off a sudden insight from the observation that prompted it. He is sparing with commas in the Journal, and rarely uses a semicolon. He is not at all averse to a sentence fragment. The style of his Journal is in fact startlingly modern.

Thoreau's spelling, though erratic, is also more modern and more American than Torrey and Allen made it appear. Where Thoreau wrote "today" and "tonight," Torrey and Allen made it "to-day" and "to-night." Where Thoreau wrote "cornfield" and "cardinal flower," Torrey and Allen made it "corn-field" and "cardinal-flower." They Britishized some spellings, changing "center" to "centre" and "gray" to "grey." They consolidated many short paragraphs and added many exclamation points, giving the text an effusive tone that is sometimes unwarranted. I have reversed these changes and chosen standard spellings where variants appear in the original (for example, "catnip" rather than "catnep").

In some cases I have preferred a reading in the 1906 edition to one in the Princeton edition. For instance, for June 22, 1851, the 1906 editors have, "The tall buttercup stars the meadow on another side, telling of the wealth of dairies." The Princeton editors replace "dairies" with "daisies." This might seem a more sensible reading, except that a year later, in a passage about cowslips, Thoreau speculates that the yellow blossom of the cowslip colors the butter of the dairy cows that eat it. If cowslips suggested dairies to Thoreau, it seems likely that buttercups (and perhaps butter-and-eggs) suggested them as well. Similarly, the 1906 edition for September 28, 1851, has this: "Though the moss is comparatively dry, I cannot walk without upsetting the numerous pitchers, which are now full of water, and so wetting my feet." The Princeton edition makes this "the moist is comparatively dry," a reading I find unlikely—not only because it makes for peculiar English but because in the previous sentence Thoreau mentions walking over coarse reddish moss.

Thoreau as Botanist

RAY ANGELO

Ray Angelo is widely considered the foremost authority on the historical flora of Concord. From 1974 to 1998 he was associated with Harvard University's Concord Field Station in Bedford, Massachusetts. From 1979 to 1984 he was assistant curator of vascular plants for the New England Botanical Club, and from 1984 to 2008 he served as curator. Since 1990 he has been an associate of the Harvard University Herbaria. Angelo is nearing the completion of his work with Dr. David Boufford on an atlas of the flora of New England (http://ne atlas.org/), and he is a regional reviewer for the Flora of North America project.

Between 2012 and 2014, Angelo compiled his field and scholarly research on Concord's flora and published online "The Vascular Flora of Concord, Massachusetts," the most comprehensive floral history of Concord to date. His related publications include "Two Thoreau Letters at Harvard," "Thoreau's Climbing Fern Rediscovered," Concord Area Trees and Shrubs, *the* Botanical Index to the Journal of Henry David Thoreau, Edward S. Hoar Revealed, *and* In Memoriam: Richard Jefferson Eaton. *Angelo's article documenting the recent status of 192 Concord plant species, "Review of Claims of Species Loss in the Flora of Concord, Massachusetts, Attributed to Climate Change," appeared in the online journal* Phytoneuron *2014–84: 1–48.*

"Thoreau as Botanist" first appeared in 1984, in both the Thoreau Quarterly, *issue 15, and the* Botanical Index to the Journal of Henry David Thoreau *(Salt Lake City: Gibbs Smith). An online version of the* Botanical Index *is available at www.ray-a.com/ThoreauBotIdx/.*

Thoreau was not the first to botanize in Concord, Massachusetts. Two brothers, Drs. Edward and Charles Jarvis, of the generation before him, collected many specimens in the town before Henry had graduated from Harvard. Thoreau certainly was not the last to botanize here. His writings have fueled an interest in the flora of Concord that extends uninterrupted over a century and a half to the present day. There is probably no other township in New England that has had such long-standing and continuous attention devoted to its plants. Adorned with rivers, lush meadows, ponds, bogs, and calcareous cliffs, the venerable settlement has rewarded botanists with a floral variety unmatched, perhaps, by any other area in New England of comparable size (1,190 species and counting).

The beginnings of Thoreau's exposure to the science of botany date back to his schooldays at the Concord Academy (1828–33), where botany was one of the disciplines taught by Phineas Allen. Also at this time he attended lectures at the Concord Lyceum, which included botany among other topics. When Thoreau attended Harvard (1833–37) botany was not offered as a course in itself, but was included under natural history taught by the noted entomologist Thaddeus W. Harris. About this time a boarder with the Thoreau family, Prudence Ward, shared with him her interest in botanical studies. Thoreau later recollected (Dec. 4, 1856, *Journal*) that during this period he began to use Jacob Bigelow's *Florula Bostoniensis, a Collection of Plants of Boston and Its Vicinity* (no doubt the second edition of 1824). Primarily he was looking for popular names of plants and references to localities. Since he used no system, the Latin names he learned at this time were soon forgotten.

Upon graduation from Harvard Thoreau did some schoolteaching in his native town. Natural history was one of the subjects he taught. He told his pupils that he knew the blossoming times of the local flowers well enough that he could determine what month it was by what was in flower. In 1842 he was asked to review for *The Dial* a series of natural history reports commissioned by the Commonwealth of Massachusetts. Included in the series was Rev. Chester Dewey's *Report on the Herbaceous Plants of Massachusetts*. The ostensible review, entitled "Natural History of Massachusetts," does not include a single Latin plant name, perhaps intentionally. Thoreau's concern was that mere lists of plants (which Dewey's work essentially was) were an inadequate expression of the state's floral resources. At this time Thoreau's botanical knowledge was insufficiently scientific for him to comment in detail on the technical merits of the report had he wanted to. Moreover, he had not traveled widely enough in Massachusetts to judge its completeness.

What survives of Thoreau's *Journal* and correspondence from the 1840s shows little stirring in the direction of scientific botany. In a letter to his sister Sophia on May 22, 1843, from Staten Island he writes, "Tell Miss Ward I shall try to put my microscope to a good use, and if I find any new and pressible flower, will throw it into my common place book." Thoreau's first use of a Latin name for a plant appears to be in his *Journal* (vol. 2, p. 9, Princeton edition) where he refers to "Mikania scandens," climbing hempweed, on September 12, 1842. This same passage in slightly modified form appears in Thoreau's *A Week* in 1849 (p. 44, Princeton edition).

The first use by Thoreau of a scientific name for a native plant in his published work appears to occur in 1848. The name "pinus nigra" is found in the original version of the Ktaadn essay that appeared in the *Union Magazine of Literature and Art* of that year. This was the name for black spruce (*Picea mariana*) used in Bigelow's manual. In a later version of the text Thoreau changed the name to that used in Asa Gray's manual, namely "*Abies nigra,*" and also inserted an additional Latin name, "*Vaccinium vitis-idaea.*" Thoreau's background in classical languages and his delight in etymology naturally attracted him to the Latin (and Greek) names of science.

Two events in the later 1840s played a major role in stimulating Thoreau's interest in systematic natural history. The first was the arrival in 1846 of a "true giant" in the realm of science at the time—naturalist Louis Agassiz, who accepted an appointment at Harvard. As A. Hunter Dupree has noted: "Not only his attainments but his remarkable personality created a sensation among the local scientists." The very next year Thoreau's correspondence with Agassiz's assistant, James Elliot Cabot, included frequent use of scientific nomenclature to discuss the collection of animal specimens.

The second event, which more directly crystallized Thoreau's botanical inclinations, was the publication in 1848 of the first edition of Asa Gray's *Manual of Botany.* The appearance of this work heralded the end of a long period during which New England botany had languished at a relatively rudimentary level. This manual for the identification of vascular plants, mosses, and liverworts of the northeastern United States was as dry as Dewey's report and Bigelow's manual, but it was far more comprehensive and accurate.

Two years earlier George B. Emerson's *Report on Trees and Shrubs Growing Naturally in the Forests of Massachusetts* had appeared. This work, while much more limited in scope, devoted more attention to the occurrence and usefulness of each species than any previous manual, and its descriptions were more detailed. Both Gray's manual and Emerson's report made use of a natural system to arrange their species rather than the artificial system of Linnaeus adopted by Bigelow. The availability of these two volumes, which were unlike any that had come before in New England, could not help but encourage a more systematic study of plants by Thoreau.

Thoreau's first work touching upon natural history after these events was *A Week on the Concord and Merrimack Rivers,* published in 1849. In this book Thoreau finally injects a measured dose of Latin nomenclature into his nature writing, particularly with respect to fishes. Agassiz is even mentioned. Thoreau's application of scientific names to plants, however, is sparing—limited to eight plants, all of them relatively common and easy to distinguish.

In the 1906 edition of Thoreau's *Journal* the first Latin name for a native plant occurs in an entry for May 1850—"Prunus depressa" (now *Prunus susquehanae,* sand cherry). From August 31 of this year onward, the use of scientific plant names becomes a regular feature of the spring, summer, and autumn pages of the *Journal*. Thoreau recalled later (Dec. 4, 1856, *Journal*) that this was about the time he returned to the study of plants with more method. The year 1850 is also that to which the earliest specimens in his organized herbarium belong.

Over the next two or three years Thoreau undertook an intensive program to develop his mastery of Concord's flora. He read botanical works by François André Michaux, Edward Tuckerman, John Loudon, Asa Gray, and Carolus Linnaeus. In his *Journal* he noted comparisons of the artificial Linnaean ordering of plants with natural systems, but always with the comment that neither addressed the poetical aspects of plants. When he sought the literature rather than the science of plants he was told to his dismay, by naturalist and Harvard librarian Thaddeus W. Harris, that he had already read all there was.

His efforts in the field during these years produced complaints of too much observation:

> I have the habit of attention to such excess that my senses get no rest, but suffer from constant strain. . . . When I have found my-self ever looking down and confining my gaze to the flowers, I have thought it might be well to get into the habit of observing the clouds as a corrective; but no! that study would be just as bad. (Sept. 13, 1852, *Journal*)

> I feel that I am dissipated by so many observations. . . . I have almost a slight, dry headache as the result of all this observing. (March 23, 1853, *Journal*)

In the winter of 1852, when there were no flowers to observe, he under-took the study of lichens.

Not surprisingly, the conflict between Thoreau the Artist and Thoreau the Naturalist began to surface: "What sort of science is that which en-riches the understanding, but robs the imagination?" (Dec. 25, 1851, *Jour-nal*); "I have become sadly scientific" (July 13, 1852, Letter to Sophia Thoreau).

It is somewhat startling to realize what Thoreau did *not* know at the start of his program in 1850—particularly with respect to woody plants. Thoreau, three years after his stay at Walden Pond, had never distinguished the first native tree to blossom in spring, silver maple (*Acer saccharinum*) (May 1, 1852, *Journal*); was unaware that but one type of spruce, black spruce (*Picea mariana*), occurred in Concord (May 25, 1857, *Journal*); could not distinguish poison ivy (*Rhus radicans*) from poison sumac (*Rhus vernix*) (May 25, 1851, *Journal*); and did not know the common witherod (*Viburnum cassinoides*) (Sept. 11, 1851, *Journal*). Thoreau later recalled this state of ignorance:

> I remember gazing with interest at the swamps about those days and wondering if I could ever attain to such familiarity with plants

that I should know the species of every twig and leaf in them, that I should be acquainted with every plant (excepting grasses and cryptogamous ones), summer and winter, that I saw. Though I knew most of the flowers, and there were not in any particular swamp more than half a dozen shrubs that I did not know, yet these made it seem like a maze to me, of a thousand strange species, and I even thought of commencing at one end and looking it faithfully and laboriously through till I knew it all. I little thought that in a year or two I should have attained to that knowledge without all that labor. (December 4, 1856, *Journal*)

During the early 1850s Thoreau's passion for recording flowering dates and leafing of woody plants dawns. He described the great lengths he went to at times to ascertain the exact date a particular flower opened—"running to different sides of the town and into neighboring towns, often between twenty and thirty miles in a day" (Dec. 4, 1856, *Journal*). Understandably, he noted: "One has as much as he can do to observe how flowers successively unfold" (June 15, 1852, *Journal*). His fascination for flowering dates never abated. It was always a victory to discover a new station for a plant with an earlier blossom time: "It will take you half a lifetime to find out where to look for the earliest flower" (April 2, 1856, *Journal*). In his last years Thoreau organized this and other phenological data spanning a decade into elaborate monthly charts. These may represent the skeleton of a contemplated volume portraying a representative year in Concord.

As Thoreau's botanical acumen rapidly developed, he accepted the role of town botanist. It was important to him to know the location of plants rare in Concord. He made one of his most noteworthy finds while surveying in November 1851—the climbing fern (*Lygodium palmatum*), a peculiarly attractive fern that is regionally scarce. In May 1853 he discovered the showy painted-cup (*Castilleja coccinea*) and marveled "how long some very conspicuous ones [flowers] may escape the most diligent walker, if you do not chance to visit their localities the right week or fortnight." In the same month he related in the *Journal* an amusing account of extracting the locality of the fragrant roseshell azalea (*Rhododendron roseum*) or pinxter-flower from a local hunter. He saw allegorical significance in the fact "that, when I thought I knew the flowers so well, the beautiful purple azalea or pinxter-flower should be shown me by the hunter who found it" (May 31, 1853, *Journal*). Part of his argument used to persuade the hunter, Melvin, was that "I was a botanist and ought to know."

Thoreau's botanical interest in Concord naturally overflowed into his travels away from his native township. The accounts of his earliest significant trips—*Ktaadn and the Maine Woods* (1848), *A Week* (1849), and *An Excursion to Canada* (1853)—contain for the most part references only to common plants with relatively little use of Latin names. The same is essentially true for *Walden* (1854). A trip to Mt. Wachusett, Massachusetts in October 1854 is represented in his *Journal* primarily by a list of common names of trees and shrubs seen there. This is a forerunner of more extensive lists, primarily in Latin, prepared for later excursions. For example, plants collected on a journey to Vermont and New Hampshire in September 1856 were carefully listed in the *Journal*. Similarly, notes in the *Journal* on his July 1855 trip to Cape Cod are littered with the Latin names for those flowers peculiar to the coast. By contrast, his articles on Cape Cod that appeared in *Putnam's Magazine* that year contain only two scientific plant names.

By 1857 Thoreau had clearly progressed beyond the fledgling stage and was perhaps one of the more competent amateur botanists in Massachusetts. In this year he made one of the most detailed lists of plants recorded for one of his journeys—the Allegash trip to Maine. This occurs in the *Journal* (not published in the 1906 edition) and as an appendix to *Maine Woods* (1864). This list also notes species seen on his Chesuncook trip to Maine in September 1853.

In July 1858 Thoreau made possibly his most significant contribution to New England botany. That month he ascended Mt. Washington, New Hampshire—the highest peak in New England—and prepared the most detailed list of plants by zones that had ever been made for this site, one not to be surpassed until the twentieth century. The month before he had similarly listed plants found on Mt. Monadnock, New Hampshire; he supplemented this list with more botanical notes after a return visit in August 1860. The listing of plants by zones was probably inspired by Alexander von Humboldt's famous correlation of altitudinal plant zones with those of latitude.

Thoreau's journey to Minnesota in 1861 was made at a time when his botanical prowess was considerable but when his health was failing. His enthusiastic companion, Horace Mann, Jr., was a young naturalist whose promising career in botany at Harvard was cut short by tuberculosis within the decade. Thoreau's notebooks for the journey are liberally sprinkled with scientific plant names—old friends and new. Included also were the customary lists of plants seen. This was to be essentially Thoreau's last botanical foray.

Although Thoreau demonstrated much botanical curiosity on his excursions, it was always Concord's flora that was dearest to him: "Many a weed here stands for more of life to me than the big trees of California would if I should go there" (Nov. 20, 1857, *Journal*). On February 4, 1858, Thoreau was astonished to find Labrador tea (*Ledum groenlandicum*) in Concord. He had, however, anticipated the discovery a year and a half earlier: "But why should not as wild plants grow here as in Berkshire, as in Labrador? . . . I shall never find in the wilds of Labrador any greater wildness than in some recess in Concord" (Aug. 30, 1856, *Journal*).

In the same swamp that harbored the Labrador tea, Thoreau noticed some curious growth on the black spruce there. Here he missed the opportunity to describe a plant at that time unknown to science: the locally rare parasite, dwarf mistletoe (*Arceuthobium pusillum*).

Starting about 1858 Thoreau undertook the study of grasses and sedges in earnest. These groups are relatively unfamiliar even to most modern botanists. Within two or three years he attained a substantial knowledge of those species that occur in Concord. His collections include nearly 100 species from the township (nearly half of those recorded in the town to date). Other difficult plant groups such as lichens, mosses, and fungi resisted study owing to the absence of good regional manuals. Consequently, excepting lichens, his scientific references to these plant groups are minimal. Even with lichens he never came close to acquiring expertise comparable to what he achieved with vascular plants. In a short article entitled "Thoreau, the Lichenist" lichenologist Reginald Heber Howe, Jr., commented that Thoreau's observations of lichens showed "only a slight knowledge of species, and no technical grasp whatsoever." But Howe, who studied lichens in Concord about sixty years after Thoreau, noted that Thoreau knew the varied morphological types and appreciated their place in Nature. (See *The Guide to Nature*, vol. 5, pp. 17–20, 1912.) Any collections he might have made of lichens, mosses, and fungi are not known to have survived.

In his day there were relatively few regional botanists for Thoreau to share his observations with. The most notable New England botanist, Asa Gray (1810–88), at Harvard, was apparently not very accessible and was known to be primarily a herbarium botanist rather than a field botanist. A. Hunter Dupree, Gray's biographer, states that neither Ralph Waldo Emerson nor Thoreau crossed Asa Gray's path and attributes this to the empiricist Gray's hostility towards Transcendentalism.

Aside from Asa Gray, virtually all other botanists in New England at this time were amateurs. The most knowledgeable of these that Thoreau met was Rev. John L. Russell (1808–73) of Salem, Massachusetts. Russell, a Unitarian minister, was for forty years professor of botany and vegetable physiology at the Massachusetts Horticultural Society and became a fellow of the American Academy of Arts and Sciences. He was well acquainted with men who described new plant species and for whom species were named. Russell was particularly interested in mosses, liverworts, and lichens. Since Russell was a classmate of Ralph Waldo Emerson's brother, Charles, at Harvard, it is likely that Thoreau first learned of Russell through Emerson. Russell visited Emerson in September 1838 at which time Emerson noted in his *Journal* that he was "A man in whose mind things stand in the order of cause & effect & not in the order of a shop or even of a cabinet."

What may have been Thoreau's first meeting with Russell occurred in Concord in August 1854. Thoreau's appetite for authoritative botanical identifications is evidenced by his notes for the three days he showed Russell around the township, which included a visit to the climbing fern. Russell made a second visit on July 23, 1856, to see a small yellow pond lily (*Nuphar* spp.). Russell must have noted Thoreau's increasing botanical proficiency and certainly was made aware of his new interest in grasses and sedges at the time of their last meeting on September 21, 1858. That day Thoreau visited Russell at Cape Ann and the Essex Institute in Salem, Massachusetts. The day was divided between a morning with the Institute's collections and an afternoon in the field. Thoreau made the most of the opportunity to confirm identifications in difficult groups like willows (*Salix*) and lichens.

Other published botanists, such as Jacob Bigelow (1787–1879), professor of materia medica at Harvard, and George B. Emerson (1797–1881), both in the Boston area, apparently moved in social circles too rarefied ever to permit personal acquaintance with Thoreau. Schoolmaster and botanist Emerson was president of the Boston Society of Natural History of which Thoreau was elected a corresponding member in 1850 (for contributing an American goshawk). According to A. Hunter Dupree, Emerson was dean of the scientific community in Boston and responsible for Asa Gray's appointment at Harvard in 1842. Though Thoreau made frequent visits to the collections and library of the Society, his interest there was primarily in fauna. Not being a regular member, he did not rub shoulders with members Gray, Bigelow, and Emerson. Consequently, Thoreau's meetings with Russell represent his closest contact with a botanist of professional caliber.

Although Benjamin Marston Watson (1820–96) was, strictly speaking, a horticulturist, his friendship with Thoreau provided an important opportunity to share botanical notes. Watson established his Old Colony Nurseries in Plymouth, Massachusetts in 1845. This estate became a favorite retreat for the Transcendentalists of Concord. Thoreau in the same year (and only one month after setting up at Walden Pond) forwarded to Watson some fruit and seeds from some of Concord's uncommon trees and shrubs. The evident purpose was to assist Watson in his horticultural enterprise. Watson in turn sent Thoreau unusual specimens from his nursery, hired him to survey his farm, and invited him to lecture in Plymouth. Thoreau's *Journal* records regular visits to Watson in Plymouth where he could see living examples of plants foreign to New England.

A mutual friend of Thoreau and Marston Watson was George P. Bradford (1807–90), a teacher, who for a time did some market gardening with Watson in Plymouth and had been part of the Brook Farm experiment. He had taught a class in botany at a school for girls in Plymouth in 1830. The references to Bradford in Thoreau's *Journal* are brief, touching primarily on unusual botanical finds. There is the suggestion that Bradford shared a Transcendentalist interest in botany when Thoreau notes Edward Hoar's proposal that a leaf of the climbing fern be sent to Bradford "to remind him that the sun still shone in America" (Aug. 14, 1854, *Journal*).

Oddly, there is but one inconsequential reference to Bradford in Thoreau's published correspondence.

Bradford, Russell, and Austin Bacon of Natick are acknowledged in the preface to George B. Emerson's report on the trees and shrubs of Massachusetts. This preface approximates a directory of Massachusetts botanists in 1846. Austin Bacon (1813–88) was a surveyor-naturalist. Thoreau paid a visit to him on August 24, 1857, and was shown a number of Natick's botanical highlights. Thoreau's interest in Natick no doubt arose from his reading of Oliver N. Bacon's *History of Natick,* which included a list of unusual plants (Jan. 19, 1856, *Journal*).

Among Concordians there were only Edward S. Hoar, Minot Pratt, and sister Sophia with whom Thoreau spoke about botany in any depth. Edward S. Hoar (1823–93), a retired lawyer, accompanied Thoreau on his trips to the White Mountains of New Hampshire and Maine's Allegash and Penobscot Rivers. He was also Thoreau's accomplice in the accidental burning of the Fairhaven Woods in Concord in 1844. Like Thoreau, Hoar collected plant specimens and pressed them. Indeed, Hoar's collections are much superior in quality, particularly with respect to the legibility and detail of his collection data. The majority of his specimens were collected from 1857–60 and included many grasses and sedges. These were the years during which Thoreau undertook a study of the same difficult groups, but curiously the *Journal* offers no support for the idea that they studied together. The references to Hoar in the *Journal* do show that Hoar brought to Thoreau's attention various botanical curiosities that he found. It is evident that for Thoreau's northern journeys Hoar was the companion of choice because of his enthusiasm for natural history, particularly of the botanical variety.

Minot Pratt (1805–78), a farmer-horticulturist, moved to Concord after four years at the Brook Farm experiment. If there was anyone as intimately familiar with Concord's wild flowers as Thoreau, it was Minot Pratt. Apparently he was just as independent since Thoreau's references to him in the *Journal* suggest only limited communication between the two about the location of Concord's rarities. On three occasions Pratt gave Thoreau a botanical tour of his neck of the woods—Punkatasset Hill and Estabrook Woods, some of the richest areas in the town botanically (Aug. 17, 1856; May 18, 1857; and June 7, 1857, *Journal*). Pratt later engaged in a practice that has earned him a degree of notoriety among latter-day botanists, namely the establishment of alien plants in Concord. Thoreau rarely did the same, but his introduction of *Nasturtium officinale* is an example (April 26, 1859, *Journal*).

Judging from her herbarium now at the Concord Free Public Library, Sophia Thoreau (1819–76) had an interest in botany that was considerably less scientific than her brother's and more in the aesthetic vein. Many of her pressed plants consist of several species to a sheet with an eye to attractive arrangement. There is rarely any information recorded as to their identity or location. Thoreau mentions three flowers in his sister's herbarium that he had not seen in Concord—whorled pogonia (*Isotria verticillata*), painted trillium (*Trillium undulatum*), and perfoliate bellwort (*Uvularia perfoliata*) (Sept. 22, 1852, *Journal*). All are locally rare. Strangely, there is no evidence that Thoreau ever saw any of these within the bounds of Concord (where Sophia found them). This suggests a bit of sibling rivalry.

The general scarcity of botanists in New England in Thoreau's time undoubtedly arose from a virtual absence of illustrated manuals and popular field guides treating the flora of the region. These were to appear only later in the nineteenth century. Thoreau complained of this lack (compared to what the British had) indirectly: "A few pages of cuts representing the different parts of plants, with the botanical names attached, is worth volumes of explanation" (Feb. 17, 1852, *Journal*). He found the plant descriptions available unsatisfactory, and they *were:* "I quarrel with most botanists' description of different species, say of willows . . . No stress is laid upon the peculiarity of the species in question, and it requires a very careful examination and comparison to detect any difference in the description" (May 25, 1853, *Journal*); "You cannot surely identify a plant from a scientific description until after long practice" (April 26, 1857, Letter to B. B. Wiley).

Thoreau's library (as listed by Walter Harding in 1957) reflects the relative dearth of botanical references of the time. He owned almost all the volumes that would pertain to Concord's vascular flora and a number that were only marginally relevant. Walter Harding's catalog includes the following botanical works:

Handbook of Plants & Fruits of the Vegetable Kingdom (Chapin)
Massachusetts Zoological and Botanical Survey (Dewey and Emmons)

Report on Trees and Shrubs Growing Naturally in the Forests of Massachusetts (Emerson)

Culture of the Grass (Flint)

Manual of Botany, 1st and 2nd eds. (Gray)

Popular History of British Lichens (Lindsay)

Arboretum et Fruticum Brittanicum (Loudon)

Encyclopedia of Plants (Loudon)

Sive Enchiridion Botanicum, or a Complete Herbal (Lovell)

The Ferns of Great Britain (Sowerby)

A Popular History of British Mosses (Stark)

To this list should be added Jacob Bigelow's *Florula Bostoniensis* (various editions), which Thoreau must have owned judging from the frequent
Journal references to it. Three well-known manuals that Thoreau consulted
from time to time were Amos Eaton's *A Manual of Botany for the Northern and Middle States* (various editions), John Torrey's *Flora of the Northern and Middle Sections of the United States* (1826), and Torrey and Gray's
Flora of North America (1838–43). None of these offered much more than
could be found in the manuals of Bigelow and Gray. Torrey and Gray's
work was the most thorough of the three but was unfinished and covered
too much geographical territory to be convenient. If modern field guides
and botanical manuals had been available to Thoreau, his expertise would
have developed much earlier and much more rapidly. It is surprising that
he managed as well as he did.

A well-identified herbarium is the ultimate all-season botanical reference work. Unfortunately, regional herbaria were also in their infancy in
Thoreau's time. It is understandable that Thoreau did not miss the opportunity to examine the meager plant collections at the Boston Society of
Natural History rooms (June 19, 1856, *Journal*) and the Essex Institute
(Sept. 21, 1858, *Journal*). The best collections, however, were in the custody
of individuals and were private.

Thoreau's own herbarium (numbering in the end more than 900 specimens) was no doubt one of the larger collections in eastern Massachusetts
at the time. Thoreau himself realized this, commenting in a letter to Mary
Brown (April 23, 1858): "I should be glad to show you my Herbarium,
which is very large." From a modern viewpoint the data he recorded for

his collections are, on the whole, poor. Approximately one-half of the specimens note only the identity of the plant, omitting the most important bit of information — the locality. This detracts significantly from the scientific value of the collection. In the difficult groups like grasses, sedges, and willows his data are generally much better than the remainder of the collection but frequently difficult to decipher (written small, in pencil, and hurriedly or carelessly). His habit of using his straw hat as a botany box to bring home plants collected in the field tended to encourage the gathering of small, inadequate, or incomplete samples.

Thoreau evidently started his organized herbarium (as opposed to casual collections placed in commonplace books or manuals) about 1850, judging from the earliest dated specimens. This was the same period when he began to study botany with more method. Clearly Thoreau created his herbarium as an aid in sorting out the identities of plants he found in Concord and on his travels and not as a vehicle for preserving his memory among future botanists (a common purpose of private herbaria).

The disposition of his herbarium following his death was that, at his request, about 100 grasses and sedges were given to his botanical companion, Edward Hoar, and the remainder (some 800 specimens) were given to the Boston Society of Natural History. Thoreau's grasses and sedges in the possession of Hoar, along with most of Hoar's own collection, were eventually given to the New England Botanical Club by Hoar's daughter, Mrs. M. L. B. Bradford, in 1912. The Club's herbarium is presently housed at Harvard University. The Thoreau specimens have been carefully mounted on standard-sized herbarium sheets together with Thoreau's pencil-scribbled scraps of data and Hoar's transcription of them. The specimens are being cataloged and photocopied before being reincorporated into the Club's holdings. This is the most scientifically useful part of Thoreau's herbarium owing to the presence of collection data, the difficulty of the plant families involved, and the addition of annotations by later botanical experts such as M. L. Fernald.

The bulk of Thoreau's herbarium stayed with the Boston Society of Natural History until 1880 when it was given to the Concord Free Public Library. In 1959 the Library turned the collection over to Harvard University's Gray Herbarium where it resides presently separate from their main collection. Unlike Thoreau's grasses and sedges, this part of the collection appears for the most part to be in the condition in which he left it at his death. Because of its relative inaccessibility and lesser scientific value, it has received relatively little critical attention by later botanists. The specimens are somewhat insecurely attached with pieces of tape to elephant folio-sized sheets of flimsy paper. Occasionally smaller sheets of paper are used. There is usually more than one specimen to a sheet, sometimes six or more, and frequently more than one species to a page. Typically, only the Latin name for the species is written in pencil near the specimen. Locality data such as "Truro '55," "Brattleboro," or "Maine '57," are sometimes noted in pencil beside particular specimens or scribbled on small scraps of paper slipped under the specimens. The sheets are numbered in pencil and arranged in systematic order according to Gray's *Manual of Botany* (second edition). The collection is divided into six parts, each kept in a large, worn cardboard portfolio. A listing of species was made by the Boston Society of Natural History in a separate notebook.

In contrast to his sister's herbarium, Thoreau's collection is well organized and the placement of specimens on the sheets is determined by practicality rather than aesthetics. In spite of some careless handling and neglect, the specimens at present are generally in good condition. There is surprisingly little evidence of insect damage. A few specimens retain enough of their original bright tints that they appear to have been pressed within the past year. The fragility of the collection will continue to leave it vulnerable to inadvertent mistreatment by those unfamiliar with the proper manner of handling pressed specimens.

Within his lifetime Thoreau published but one work concerned with the world of plants. This is his essay "The Succession of Forest Trees," delivered as an address before the Middlesex Agricultural Society in Concord in September 1860 and published the following month in the *New York Tribune* and in regional agricultural reports. It is properly regarded as a contribution to ecology rather than to botany, but is, perhaps, his most important scientific work (representing not so much original ideas as an original development and formulation of ideas).

Thoreau's essays "Autumnal Tints" and "Wild Apples," derived from his *Journal* and presented as lectures, were revised during the last months of his life and published posthumously in the *Atlantic Monthly* in 1862. These essays are part of Thoreau's attempt to fill a void that he felt existed in the literature of botany. When he first began his study of plants in earnest he had sought out "those works which contained the more particular *popular* account, or *biography,* of particular flowers, . . . for I trusted that each flower had had many lovers and faithful describers in past times" (Feb. 6, 1852, *Journal*). "Autumnal Tints" and "Wild Apples" present an aesthetic appreciation of plants. While grounded in science, the essays are in fact examples of literature.

Among the fragmentary manuscripts left by Thoreau are what appear to be a series of essays he was working on with titles "Wild Fruit," "The Dispersion of Seeds," "The Fall of the Leaf," and "New England Native Fruits." From these manuscripts Leo Stoller has pieced together an essay entitled "Huckleberries," the style and content of which very much parallels "Autumnal Tints" and "Wild Apples." A key phrase in the essay is "The berries *which I celebrate*" (italics Thoreau's), indicating the spirit intended in these pieces.

Thoreau's studies in botany did not result in significant contributions to the science of botany. Most New England botanists would be hard pressed to identify his most important botanical achievement—the first detailed description of the vegetation zones on New England's highest peak, Mt. Washington. Although the description was not published until well after his death, his observations provide a point of comparison that reveals changes in alpine vegetation at New England's most interesting botanical site.

Thoreau's extensive study of the plants of Concord also serves as a point of comparison for noting changes in the flora. It is important for this reason, rather than for resulting in particular botanical finds in Concord. His observations and collections in Concord represent, perhaps, the most complete survey of a New England township's flora up to that time. Thoreau in essence has provided later botanists with a "photograph" of Concord's flora in the 1850s. None of Concord's other botanists have matched the intensity of activity that engaged him during that decade. His plant identifications (once he passed beyond the novice stage) were very competent, with doubts or errors occurring only at those points where the professional botanists themselves (and their manuals) were confused. Thoreau's intimate familiarity with the location of unusual plants in Concord was equaled only by Minot Pratt. The breadth of Thoreau's botanical knowledge (which included grasses, sedges, and lichens) has been approached only by Edward Hoar and the late Richard J. Eaton of the twentieth century.

It was not Thoreau's aim to add to the body of botanical knowledge of his time. Rather, his efforts arose from a desire to distinguish more clearly the textures with which Nature clothed his native town, and his New England, since he felt himself to be part of the same fabric: "I am interested in each contemporary plant in my vicinity, and have attained to a certain acquaintance with the larger ones. They are cohabitants with me of this part of the planet, and they bear familiar names" (June 5, 1857, *Journal*). Domesticated plants were of little or no interest to him: "I was never in the least interested in plants in the house" (Dec. 4, 1856, *Journal*). His early attention to flowers was coincident with the general Transcendentalist view of Nature—as a source of inspiration, a living lesson from which to extract a moral, an invitation to experience rather than an opportunity to analyze. Later, his systematic approach to plants was undertaken with philosophical discomfort and ensuing rationalization: "Once I was part and parcel of Nature; now I am observant of her" (April 2, 1852, *Journal*); "One studies the books of science merely to learn the language of naturalists—to be able to communicate with them" (March 23, 1853, *Journal*). To the end he considered himself not a naturalist or botanist but a writer, first and foremost: "Here I have been these forty years learning the language of these fields that I may the better express myself" (Nov. 20, 1857, *Journal*). Yet, for a writer to acquaint himself so completely and consciously with the flora of his native region was unprecedented, and inspires wonder as to what grand work of prose this insistent pursuit of botany was meant to nurture.

thoreau's wildflowers

The snow has melted very rapidly the past week. There is much bare ground. The checkerberries are revealed—*somewhat* shriveled many of them. . . . In Hubbard's maple swamp I see the evergreen leaves of the gold-thread as well as the mitchella and large pyrola. I begin to snuff the air and smell the ground. In the meadow beyond I see some still fresh and perfect pitcher plant leaves and everywhere the green and reddish radical leaves of the golden senecio, whose fragrance when bruised carries me back or forward to an incredible season. Who would believe that under the snow and ice lie still, or in midwinter, some green leaves which bruised yield the same odor that they do when their yellow blossoms spot the meadows in June? Nothing so realizes the summer to me now.

partridgeberry (*Mitchella repens*)

golden ragwort
(*Senecio aureus=Packera aurea*)

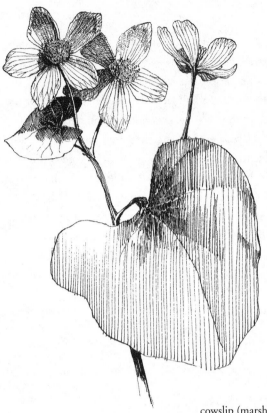

cowslip (marsh marigold, *Caltha palustris*)

MARCH 5, 1859

Those skunk cabbage buds which are most advanced have cast off their outermost and often frostbitten sheaths, and the spathe is broader and slightly opened (some three quarters of an inch or more already) and has acquired brighter and more variegated colors. The outside of the spathe shows some ripeness in its colors and markings like a melon rind before the spadix begins to bloom. I find that many of the most forward spathes, etc., have been destroyed since I was here three days ago. Some animal has nibbled away a part of the spathes (or sometimes only a hole in it) — and I see the fragments scattered about — and then eaten out the whole of the spadix. Indeed but few forward ones are left. Is this a mouse — or musquash — or a bird? The spadix is evidently a favorite titbit to some creature. . . .

The cowslip there [Well Meadow] is very prominently flower-budded, lifting its yellow flower buds above water in one place. The leaves are quite inconspicuous when they first come up, being rolled up tightly.

MARCH 6, 1859

The slender black birches with their catkined twigs gracefully drooping on all sides are very pretty. Like the alders with their reddish catkins they express more life than most trees. Most trees look completely at rest if not dead now—but these look as if the sap must be already flowing in them (and in winter as well).

MARCH 7, 1854

It is remarkable how true each plant is to its season. Why should not the fringed gentian put forth early in the spring instead of holding in till the latter part of September? I do not perceive enough difference in the temperature. How short a time it is with us!

MARCH 7, 1859

The mystery of the life of plants is kindred with that of our own lives, and the physiologist must not presume to explain their growth according to mechanical laws or mechanics of his own making. We must not expect to probe with our fingers the sanctuary of life whether animal or vegetable. If we do we shall discover nothing but surface still.

MARCH 8, 1855

As the ice melts in the swamps I see the horn-shaped buds of the skunk cabbage, green with a bluish bloom, standing uninjured, ready to feel the influence of the sun. The most prepared for spring—to look at—of any plant.

skunk cabbage (*Symplocarpus foetidus*)

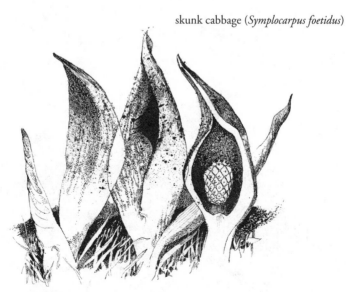

I see the reticulated leaves of the rattlesnake plantain in the woods, quite fresh and green. What is the little chickweed-like plant already springing up on the top of the Cliffs? There are some other plants with bright green leaves which have either started somewhat or have never suffered from the cold under the snow. Summer clenches hands with summer under the snow.

downy rattlesnake-plantain
(*Goodyera pubescens*)

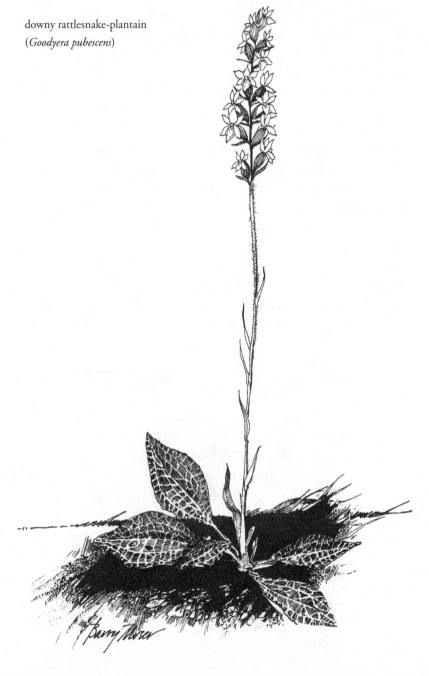

MARCH 10, 1853

Many plants are to some extent evergreen, like the buttercup now beginning to start. Methinks the first obvious evidence of spring is the pushing
out of the swamp willow catkins, then the relaxing of the earlier alder catkins, then the pushing up of skunk cabbage spathes (and pads at the bottom of water). This is the order I am inclined to, though perhaps any of
these may take precedence of all the rest in any particular case.

MARCH 10, 1855

Observed this afternoon some celandine by Deacon Brown's fence, apparently grown about an inch. *Vide* if it is really springing.

celandine (*Chelidonium majus*)

MARCH 12, 1853

The sweet gale is the prettiest flower which I have [found] expanded yet.
. . . Was that a mink we saw at the Boiling Spring? The senecio was very
forward there in the water, and it still scents my fingers—a very lasting
odor it leaves.

MARCH 14, 1855

I observe the tracks of sparrows leading to every little sprig of bluecurls
amid the other weeds, which, its seemingly *empty* pitchers, rises above the
snow. There seems however to be a little seed left in them. This then is
reason enough why these withered stems still stand—that they may raise
these granaries above the snow for the use of the snow birds.

sweet gale (*Myrica gale*)

MARCH 16, 1860

The buttercup radical leaves are many of them now a healthy dark green, as if they had acquired new life. I notice that such are particularly downy— and probably that enables them to endure the cold so well, like mulleins. Those and thistles and shepherd's purse, etc., have the form of rosettes on the brown ground.

MARCH 17, 1857

No mortal is alert enough to be present at the first dawn of the spring— but he will presently discover some evidence that vegetation had awaked some days at least before.

MARCH 18, 1853

It is decidedly clearing up. At Conantum Cliff the columbines have started and the saxifrage even, the former as conspicuously as any plant, particularly any on dry ground. Both these grow there in high and dry chinks in the face of the cliff, where no soil appears, and the sunnier the exposure the more advanced. Even if a fallen fragment of the rock is so placed as to reflect the heat upon it, it has the start of its neighbors. These plants waste not a day, not a moment suitable to their development. I pluck dry sprigs of pennyroyal which I love to put in my pocket, for it scents me thoroughly and reminds me of garrets full of herbs.

MARCH 18, 1858

Eight or ten rods off I noticed an evergreen shrub with the aspect or habit of growth of the juniper—but as it was in the woods, I already suspected it to be what it proved, the American yew already strongly budded to bloom. This is a capital discovery. I have thus found the ledum and the taxus this winter and a new locality of the epigaea.

MARCH 18, 1860

I examine the skunk cabbage, now generally and abundantly in bloom all along under Clamshell. It is a flower as it were without a leaf. All that you see is a stout beaked hood just rising above the dead brown grass in the springy ground now—where it has felt the heat under some south bank. The single enveloping leaf or "spathe" is all the flower that you see commonly, and those are as variously colored as tulips and of similar color—

American false pennyroyal (*Hedeoma pulegioides*)

early saxifrage (*Saxifraga virginiensis=Micranthes virginiensis*)

from a very dark almost black mahogany to a light yellow streaked or freckled with mahogany. It is a leaf simply folded around the flower with its top like a bird's beak bent over it for its further protection, evidently to keep off wind and frost, with a sharp angle down its back. These various colors are seen close together, and their beaks are bent in various directions.

All along under that bank I heard the hum of honeybees in the air, attracted by this flower. Especially the hum of one within a spathe sounds deep and loud. They circle about the bud at first hesitatingly—then alight and enter at the open door and crawl over the spadix, and reappear laden with the yellow pollen. What a remarkable instinct it is that leads them to this flower.

MARCH 20, 1853

Those alder catkins on the west side of Walden tremble and undulate in the wind, they are so relaxed and ready to bloom—the most forward blossom buds. Here and there around the pond, within a rod of the water, is the fisherman's stone fireplace, with its charred brands, where he cheered and warmed himself and ate his lunch.

MARCH 21, 1855

Early willow and aspen catkins are very conspicuous now. The silvery down of the former has in some places crept forth from beneath its scales a third of an inch at least. This increased silveriness was obvious I think about the first of March, perhaps earlier. It appears to be a very gradual expansion which begins in the warm days of winter. It would be well to observe them once a fortnight through the winter. It is the first decided growth I have noticed, and is probably a month old.

MARCH 22, 1853

The very earliest alder is in bloom and sheds its pollen. This the first native flower. I detect a few catkins at a distance by their distinct yellowish color.

One of my willow catkins in the pitcher has opened at length.

MARCH 23, 1853

The buds of the shad blossom look green. The crimson starred flowers of the hazel begin to peep out though the catkins have not opened. The alders are almost generally in full bloom and a very handsome and interesting show they make with their graceful tawny pendants—inclining to yellow.

They shake like eardrops in the wind. Almost? Perhaps, the first completed ornaments with which the new year decks herself. Their yellow pollen is shaken down and colors my coat like sulphur as I go through them. I go to look for mud turtles in Heywood's meadow. The alder catkins just burst open are prettily marked spirally by streaks of yellow, contrasting with alternate rows of rich reddish brown scales—which make one revolution in the length of the catkin. . . .

The cattail down puffs and swells in your hand like a mist, or the conjurer's trick of filling a hat with feathers—for when you have rubbed off but a thimbleful and can close and conceal the wound completely, the expanded down fills your hand to overflowing. Apparently there is a spring to the fine elastic threads which compose the down which after having been so long closely packed, on being the least relieved at the base spring open apace into the form of parachutes to convey the seed afar. Where birds or the winds or ice have assaulted them this has spread like an eruption. Again when I rub off the down of the spike with my thumb I am surprised at the sensation of warmth it imparts to my hand as it flushes over it magically at the same time revealing a faint purplish crimson tinge at the base of the down as it rolls off and expands. It is a very pleasing experiment to try.

MARCH 23, 1856
I see that a shopkeeper advertises among his perfumes for handkerchiefs "meadow flowers" and "new mown hay."

MARCH 24, 1855
I think that the celandine *started* as early as the 10th of March and has since been nibbled off by hens, etc., for it shows more green but [is] not longer.

MARCH 26, 1857
The first croaking frogs, the hyla, the white maple blossoms [silver maple, *Acer saccharinum*], the skunk cabbage and the alder catkins are observed about the same time.

I saw one hazel catkin much elongated and relaxed. It is surprising always to see this on dry plains or banks where there is so little evidence of life beside.

common cattail (*Typha latifolia*)

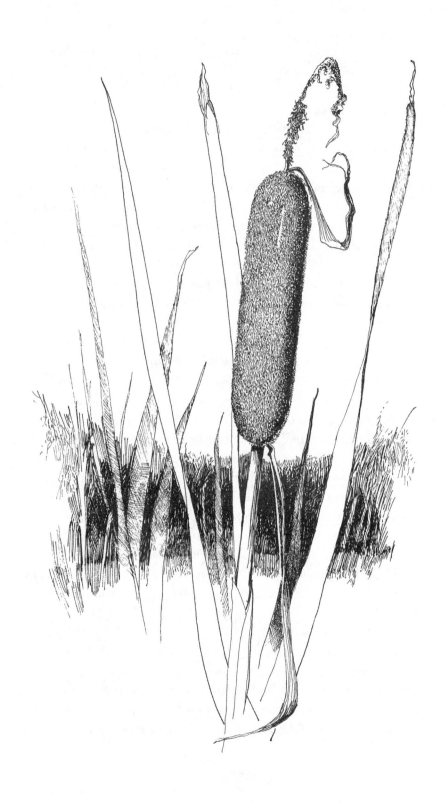

MARCH 26, 1860

The earliest willows are now in the gray, too advanced to be silvery—mouse or maltese-cat color.

MARCH 27, 1853

The hazel is fully out. The 23d was perhaps full early to date them. It is in some respects the most interesting flower yet, though so minute that only an observer of nature, or one who looked for them, would notice it. It is the highest and richest colored yet—ten or a dozen little rays at the end of the buds which are the end and along the sides of the bare stems. Some of the flowers are a light, some a dark crimson. The high color of this minute unobserved flower, at this cold leafless and almost flowerless season! It is a beautiful greeting of the spring, when the catkins are scarcely relaxed and there are no signs of life in the bush. Moreover, they are so tender that I never got one home in good condition. They wilt and turn black.

MARCH 27, 1859

There is an abundance of low willows whose catkins are now conspicuous rising four to six or seven feet above the water—thickly placed on long wand-like osiers. They look when you look from the sun like dead gray twigs or branches (whose wood is exposed) of bushes in the light—but nearer are recognized for the pretty bright buttons of the willow. We sail by masses of these silvery buttons two or three rods long, rising above the water. By their color they have relation to the white clouds and the sky and to the snow and ice still lingering in a few localities. In order to see these silvery buttons in the greatest profusion, you must sail amid them on some flooded meadow or swamp like this [Otter Bay]. Our whole course, as we wind about in this bay, is lined also with the alder whose pretty tassels now many of them in full bloom are hanging straight down, suggesting in a peculiar manner the influence of gravity, or are regularly blown one side.

It is remarkable how modest and unobtrusive these early flowers are. The musquash and duck hunter—or the farmer—might and do commonly pass by them with[out] perceiving them. They steal into the light and air of spring without being noticed for the most part. The sportsman seems to see a mass of weather-stained dead twigs showing their wood and partly covered with gray lichens and moss, and the flowers of the alder now partly in bloom, maybe half, make the impression at a little distance of a collection of the brown twigs of winter—also are of the same color with many withered leaves.

MARCH 28, 1853
Why is the pollen of flowers commonly yellow?

MARCH 28, 1858
I go down the railroad—turning off in the cut. I notice the hazel stigmas in the warm hollow on the right there *just beginning* to peep forth. This is an unobserved but very pretty and interesting evidence of the progress of the season. I should not have noticed it if I had not carefully examined the fertile buds. It is like a crimson star first dimly detected in the twilight.

MARCH 28, 1859
Our vernal lakes have a beauty to my mind which they would not possess if they were more permanent. Everything is rapid flux here [Great Meadows], suggesting that Nature is alive to her extremities and superficies. Today we sail swiftly, on dark rolling waves, or paddle over a sea as smooth as a mirror unable to touch the bottom where mowers work and hide their jugs in August—coasting the edge of maple swamp, where alder tassels and white maple flowers are kissing the tide that has risen to meet them.

MARCH 31, 1856
The celandine begins to be conspicuous, springing under Brown's fence.

APRIL 1, 1853
It has rained all night and this forenoon, and now begins to clear up. The rain rests on the downy leaves of the young mulleins in separate irregular drops, from their irregularity and color looking like ice. The drops quite in the cup of the mullein have a peculiar translucent silveriness, apparently because being upheld by the wool it reflects the light which would otherwise be absorbed. As if cased in light. The fresh mullein leaves are pushing up amid the brown unsightly wreck of last fall, which strews the ground like old clothes—these the new patches.

APRIL 1, 1858

The river is at summer level—has not been up this spring, and has fallen to this. The lowermost willow at my boat is bare. The white maples are abundantly out today. Probably the *very first* bloomed on the 29th. We hold the boat beneath one, surprised to hear the resounding hum of honeybees which are busy about them.

APRIL 2, 1856

It will take you half a lifetime to find out where to look for the earliest flower.

APRIL 3, 1853

To my great surprise the saxifrage is in bloom. It was, as it were, by mere accident that I found it. I had not observed any particular forwardness in it, when happening to look under a projecting rock in a little nook on the south side of a stump I spied one little plant which had opened three or four blossoms high up the Cliff. Evidently you must look very sharp and faithfully to find the first flower. Such is the advantage of position. And when you have postponed a flower for a week and are turning away, a little further search may reveal it.

APRIL 4, 1853

The other day when I had been standing perfectly still some ten minutes, looking at a willow which had just blossomed some rods in the rear of Martial Miles' house, I felt eyes on my back and turning round suddenly saw the heads of two men who had stolen out of the house and were watching me over a rising ground as fixedly as I the willow. They were studying Man, which is said to be the proper study of mankind, I nature, and yet when detected they felt the cheapest of the two.

APRIL 4, 1859

The epigaea looks as though it would open in two or three days at least—showing much color and this form: The flower buds are protected by the withered leaves, oak leaves, which partly cover them—so that you must look pretty sharp to detect the first flower. These plants blossom by main strength as it were, or the virtue that is in them—not growing by water as most early flowers—in dry copses.

trailing arbutus (*Epigaea repens*)

APRIL 5, 1859

As I stood on a hill just cut off I saw half a dozen rods below the bright yellow catkins of a tall willow just opened on the edge of the swamp against the dark brown twigs and the withered leaves. This early blossom looks bright and rare amid the withered leaves and the generally brown and dry surface, like the early butterflies. This is the most conspicuous of the March flowers (i.e. if it chances to be *so early* as March).

It suggests unthought-of warmth and sunniness. It takes but little color and tender growth to make miles of dry brown woodland and swamp look habitable and homelike—as if a man could dwell there.

The flower buds of the red maple have very red inner scales, now being more and more exposed, which color the treetops a great distance off. . . .

All along under the south side of this hill [Clamshell Hill] on the edge of the meadow, the air resounds with the hum of honeybees, attracted by the flower of the skunk cabbage. I first heard the fine, peculiarly sharp hum of the honeybee before I thought of them. Some hummed hollowly within the spathes, perchance to give notice to their fellows that plant was occupied—for they repeatedly looked in and backed out on finding another. . . . Some of these spathes are now quite large and twisted up like cows' horns, not curved over as usual. Commonly they make a pretty little crypt or shrine for the flower. Somewhat like this, Like the overlapping door of a tent. . . .

One cowslip, though it shows the yellow, is not *fairly* out but will be by tomorrow. How they improve their time! Not a moment of sunshine is lost.

APRIL 6, 1854

A still warmer day than yesterday—a warm moist rain-smelling west wind. I am surprised [to] find so much of the white maples already out. The light-colored stamens show to some rods. Probably they *began* as early as day before yesterday. They resound with the hum of honeybees, heard a dozen rods off, and you see thousands of them about the flowers against the sky. They know where to look for the white maple and when. This susurrus carries me forward some months toward summer.

APRIL 6, 1860

I am struck by the fact that at this season all vegetable growth is confined to the *warm* days—during the cold ones it is stationary or even killed. Vegetation thus comes forward rather by fits and starts than by a steady progress. Some flowers would blossom tomorrow if it were as warm as today, but cold weather intervening may detain them a week or more. The spring thus advances and recedes repeatedly—its pendulum oscillates while it is carried steadily forward.

APRIL 7, 1860

Early potentilla [dwarf cinquefoil, *P. canadensis*] out how long? Far side of Annursnack.

There in the slow muddy brook near the head of Well Meadow, within a few rods of its source, where it winds amid the alders which *shelter* the plants somewhat while they are *open enough* to admit the sun, I find two cowslips in full bloom, shedding pollen — and they may have opened two or three days ago; for I saw many conspicuous buds there on the second which now I do not see. Have they not been eaten off? Do we not often lose the earliest flowers thus?

The epigaea is not quite out. The earliest peculiarly *woodland* herbaceous flowers are epigaea, anemone, thalictrum, and (by the first of May) *Viola pedata* [birdfoot violet]. These grow quite in the woods amid dry leaves — nor do they depend so much on water as the very earliest flowers. I am perhaps more surprised by the growth of the *Viola pedata* leaves, by the side of paths amid the shrub oaks and half covered with oak leaves, than by any other growth. The situation is so dry and the surrounding bushes so apparently lifeless.

The *Populus tremuliformis* just beyond [Second Division Brook] *resound* with the hum of honeybees, flies, etc. These male trees are frequently at a great distance from the females. Do not the bees and flies alone carry the pollen to the latter? I did not know at first whence the humming of bees proceeded. . . .

Elm blossoms now in prime. Their tops heavier against the sky — a rich brown. Their outlines further seen. . . .

Two crowfoots out on the Cliff. A very warm and dry exposure, but no further sheltered were they. Pale yellow offering of spring. The saxifrage is beginning to be abundant, elevating its flowers somewhat. Pure trustful white amid its pretty notched and reddish cup of leaves. The white saxifrage is a response from earth to the increased light of the year — the yellow crowfoot to the increased heat of the sun. The buds of the thorn bushes are conspicuous. The chrysosplenium [golden saxifrage, *C. americanum*] is open, a few of them, in Hubbard's meadow. I thought he had destroyed them all. When the farmer cleans out his ditches, I mourn the loss of many a flower which he calls a weed. The main charm about the Corner road, just beyond the bridge, to me has been in the little grove of locusts,

quaking aspen (*Populus tremuliformis=P. tremuloides*)

sallows [willows], and birches, etc., which has sprung up on the bank as you rise the hill. Yesterday I saw a man who is building a house nearby cutting them down. I asked him if he was going to cut them all. He said he was. I said if I were in his place I would not have them cut for a hundred dollars—that they were the chief attraction of the place.

"Why," said he, "they are nothing but a parcel of prickly bushes and are not worth anything. I'm going to build a new wall here." And so to ornament the approach to his house he substitutes a bare ugly wall for an interesting grove.

APRIL 10, 1855

As for the early sedge—who would think of looking for a flower of any kind in those dry tufts whose withered blades almost entirely conceal the springing green ones? I patiently examined one tuft after another higher and higher up the rocky hill [Lee's Cliff], till at last I found one little yellow spike low in the grass—which shed its pollen on my finger. As for the saxifrage—when I had given it up for today, having after a long search in the warmest clefts and recesses found only three or four buds which showed some white—I at length on a still warmer shelf found one flower partly expanded, and its common peduncle had shot up an inch.

These few earliest flowers in these situations have the same sort of interest with the arctic flora—for they are remote and unobserved and often surrounded with snow, and most have not begun to think of flowers yet.

APRIL 10, 1859

I hear of a cinquefoil found in bloom on the 8th. It was in this [Well Meadow] sproutland, where it was protected.

This with bluets, mouse-ear, and *Viola ovata* [arrowleaf violet, *Viola sagittata* var. *ovata*] (of the herbaceous plants) I would call pasture flowers (among those of March and April).

APRIL 11, 1852

The sweet flags are now starting up under water two inches high, and minnows dart. . . . The expanding mayflower buds show a little pinkish tint under the snow. The cress is apparently all last year's. The cowslip does not yet spring.

APRIL 11, 1856

You thread your way amid the rustling oak leaves on some warm hillside sloping to the south, detecting no growth as yet unless the flower buds of the amelanchier are somewhat expanded, when glancing along the dry stems, in the midst of all this dryness, you detect the crimson stigmas of the hazel—like little stars peeping forth, and perchance a few catkins are dangling loosely in the zephyr and sprinkling their pollen on the dry leaves beneath.

APRIL 12, 1852

Saw the first blossoms (bright yellow stamens or pistils) on the willow catkins today. The speckled alders and the maples are earlier then. The yellow blossom appears first on one side of the ament and is the most of bright and sunny color the spring has shown—the most decidedly flower-like that I have seen. . . . It is fit that this almost earliest spring flower should be yellow, the color of the sun.

APRIL 13, 1852

Snowed all day till the ground was covered eight inches deep. Heard the robin singing as usual last night though it was raining. The elm buds begin to show their blossoms. As I came home through the streets at 11 o'clock last night through the snow it cheered me to think that there was a little bit of a yellow blossom by warm sandy watersides which had expanded its yellow blossom on the sunny side amid the snows. I mean the catkins of the earliest willow. To think of those little sunny spots in nature, so incredibly contrasting with all this white and cold.

APRIL 13, 1854

P.M. — Sail to Bittern Cliff.

The surface of the water, toward the sun, reflecting the light with different degrees of brilliancy is very exhilarating to look at. The red maple in a day or two. I begin to see the anthers in some buds. So much more of the scales of the buds is now uncovered that the tops of the swamps at a distance are now reddened. . . . One or two crowfoots on Lee's Cliff fully out — surprise me like a flame bursting from the russet ground.

sweet flag (*Acorus calamus*)

APRIL 13, 1855

The common hazel just out. It is perhaps the prettiest flower of the *shrubs* that have opened. A little bunch of (in this case) half a dozen catkins one and three quarters inches long trembling in the wind, shedding golden pollen on the hand—and close by as many minute but clear crystalline crimson stars at the end of a bare and seemingly dead twig. For two or three days in my walks I had given the hazel catkins a fillip with my finger under their chins to see if they were in bloom, but in vain—but here on the warm south side of a wood, I find one bunch fully out and completely relaxed. They know when to trust themselves to the weather.

speckled alder (*Alnus incana* subsp. *rugosa*)

APRIL 15, 1852

The aspen on the railroad is beginning to blossom, showing the purple or mulberry in the terminal catkins, though it droops like dead cats' tails in the rain. It appears about the same date with the elm.

APRIL 15, 1859

Consider how much is annually spent on the farmer's life—the beauty of his abode, which has inspired poets since the world was made. The hundreds of delicate and beautiful flowers scattered profusely under his feet and all around him. As he walks or drives his team afield. He cannot put his spade into uncultivated nor into much cultivated ground without disturbing some of them. A hundred or two of equally beautiful birds to sing to him—morning and evening, and some at noonday—a good part of the year. A perfect sky arched over him, a perfect carpet spread under him, etc., etc.! And can the farmer speak or think carelessly of these gifts? Will he find it in his heart to curse the flowers and shoot the birds?

APRIL 16, 1856

Golden saxifrage at Hubbard's Close.

APRIL 17, 1852

The scent of the earliest spring flowers! I smelt the willow catkins today. Tender and innocent after this rude winter, yet slightly sickening, yet full of vernal promise. This odor—how unlike anything that winter affords, or nature has afforded this six months! A mild sweet vernal scent. Not highly spiced and intoxicating, as some ere long, but attractive to bees. That early yellow smell.

APRIL 17, 1855

The flowers of the common elm at Lee's are now loose and dangling, apparently well out a day or two in advance of Cheney's, but I see no pollen. . . .

The early aspen catkins are now some of them two and a half inches long and white, dangling in the breeze. The earliest gooseberry leaves are fairly unfolding now and show some green at a little distance.

APRIL 18, 1852

What a conspicuous place nature has assigned to the skunk cabbage, first

American elm (*Ulmus americana*)

flower to show itself above the bare ground! What occult relation is implied between this plant and man? Most buds have expanded perceptibly, show some greenness or yellowness. Universally nature relaxes somewhat of her rigidity, yields to the influence of heat. Each day the grass springs and is greener. The skunk cabbage is inclosed in its spathe but the willow catkin expands its bright yellow blossoms without fear at the end of its twigs. And the fertile flower of the hazel has elevated its almost invisible crimson star of stigmas above the sober and barren earth. . . .

For the first time I perceive this spring that the year is a circle. I see distinctly the spring arc thus far. It is drawn with a firm line. Every incident is a parable of the great teacher. The cranberries washed up in the meadows and into the road on the causeways now yield a pleasant acid.

APRIL 18, 1858
A dandelion open—will shed pollen tomorrow.

APRIL 19, 1858
See two or three yellow lilies nearly open, showing most of their yellow beneath the water—say in two or three days.

APRIL 21, 1854
As I go up the hill beyond the brook [Sawmill Brook], while the hylodes are heard behind, I perceive the faintest possible flower-like scent as from the earth, reminding me of anemones and houstonias. Can it be the budded mouse-ears under my feet? Downy-swaddled, they lie along flat to the earth like a child on its mother's bosom.

APRIL 21, 1858
The puddles have dried off along the road and left thick deposits or waterlines of the dark purple anthers of the elm coloring the ground like sawdust. You could collect great quantities of them.

APRIL 22, 1855
The blossoms of the sweet gale are now on fire over the brooks, contorted like caterpillars.

APRIL 22, 1858
Andromeda, apparently a day or two (at least at edge of Island Wood, which I have not seen).

APRIL 22, 1859
I go by a *Populus grandidentata* [bigtooth aspen] on the eastern sand slope of the Deep Cut—just after entering—whose aments (which apparently *here* began to shed pollen yesterday) in scattered clusters at the ends of the bare twigs . . . not hanging loose and straight yet but curved, are a very rich crimson, like some ripe fruit—as mulberries seen against the sand. I cannot represent the number in a single cluster, but they are much the handsomest now before the crimson anthers have burst. And are all the more remarkable for the very open and bare habit of the tree.

The early luzula [common woodrush, *L. multiflora*] is almost in bloom—makes a show with its budded head and its purplish and downy silky leaves on the warm margin of Clamshell Bank. Two or three dandelions in bloom spot the ground there.

It has cleared up. At Ivy Bridge I see the honeybees entering the crypts of the skunk cabbage, whose tips have been bitten by the frost and cold. The first sweet gale, which opened a day or two ago on the sunny sides of brooks where the sun reached it above the bank, was an interesting sight, full of amber dust.

Houstonias. How affecting that annually at this season, as surely as the sun takes a higher course in the heavens, this pure and simple little flower peeps out and spots the great globe with white in our America, its four little white or bluish petals on a slender stalk making a delicate flower about a third of an inch in diameter. What a significant though faint utterance of spring through the veins of earth!

common dandelion
(*Taraxacum dens-leonis=T. officinale*)

I can find no red cedar in bloom—but it will undoubtedly shed pollen tomorrow. It is on the point of it. I am not sure that the white cedar is any earlier. The sprigs of red cedar now full of the buff colored staminate flowers like fruit are very rich. The next day they shed an abundance of pollen in the house. It is a clear buff color while that of the white cedar is very different, being a faint salmon. It would be very pleasant to make a collection of these powders like dry ground paints. They would be the right kind of chemicals to have.

The mayflower is well budded and ready to blossom, but not yet out—nor the andromeda, nor saxifrage, nor violet that I can find. I am surprised to find the cowslip in full bloom at Second Division Meadow. Numerous flowers. Growing in the water, it is not comparatively so backward this year perhaps. Its heart- or kidney-shaped crenate green leaves, which had not freshly grown when I was here before, have suddenly pushed up. The snows soon melted on this meadow. The horsetail too is ready to flower.

bluets (*Houstonia caerulea*)

black cherry (*Prunus serotina*)

APRIL 25, 1855

A moist April morning. A small native willow leafing and showing catkins today—also the black cherry in some places. The common wild rose
tomorrow. Balm of Gilead will not shed pollen apparently for a day or
more. Shepherd's purse will bloom today—the first I have noticed which
has sprung from the ground this season, or of any age. Say lilac begins to
leaf with common currant.

APRIL 25, 1857

No pages in my Journal are so suggestive as those which contain a rude
sketch.

APRIL 26, 1851

Gathered the mayflower and cowslips yesterday, and saw the houstonia,
violets, etc. Saw a dandelion in blossom.

APRIL 26, 1859

Walked with C. M. Tracy in the rain. . . . Got the *Cerastium arvense* [field chickweed] from T's garden. . . . Also got the *Nasturtium officinale* or common brook cress [watercress] from Lynn and set it in Depot Field Brook.

APRIL 26, 1860

Red maples are past prime. I have noticed their handsome crescents over distant swamps—commonly for some ten days. At height then say the *21st*. They are especially handsome when seen between you and the sunlit trees.

shepherd's purse (*Capsella bursa-pastoris*)

wild strawberry (*Fragaria virginiana*)

APRIL 27, 1855

Cold and windy—but fair. The earliest willow by railroad begins to leaf and is out of bloom. Few birds are heard this cold and windy morning.

APRIL 27, 1860

Luzula a day or two at Clamshell. Strawberry well out how long? *Viola ovata* common. One dandelion white as if going to seed!

APRIL 28, 1860

The *common Salix rostrata* [Bebb willow, *S. bebbiana*] on east side rail-road. Yesterday at least. *S. Torreyana* [wand willow, *S. eriocephala*] a day or two longer. These willows are full of bees and resound with their hum. I see honeybees laden with large pellets of the peculiar yellow pollen of the *S. rostrata*. Methinks I could tell when that was in bloom by catching the bees on their return to the hive. Here are also much smaller bees and flies, etc., etc., all attracted by these flowers. As you stand by such a willow in bloom and resounding with the hum of bees in a warm afternoon like this, you seem nearer to summer—than elsewhere.

APRIL 29, 1852

But the season is most forward at the Second Division Brook where the cowslip is in blossom and nothing yet planted at home—these bright yellow *suns* of the meadow in rich clusters, their flowers contrasting with the green leaves, from amidst the all-producing dark-bottomed water. A flower-fire bursting up as if through crevices in the meadow. They are very rich seen in the meadow where they grow, and the most conspicuous flower at present, but held in the hand are rather coarse. But their yellow and green are really rich, and in the meadow they are the most delicate objects. Their bright yellow is something incredible when first beheld.

APRIL 29, 1854

The mouse-ear is now fairly in blossom in many places. It never looks so pretty as now in an April rain, covered with pearly drops. Its corymbs of five heads with one in the center (all tinged red) look like a breastpin set with pearls.

APRIL 29, 1857

At Tarbell's watering place see a dandelion, its conspicuous bright yellow disk in the midst of a green space on the moist bank. It is thus I commonly meet with the earliest dandelion set in the midst of some liquid green patch. It seems a sudden and decided progress in the season.

APRIL 30, 1852

The elms are now generally in blossom and Cheney's elm still also. The last has leaf buds which show the white. Now before any leaves have appeared their blossoms clothe the trees with a rich warm brown color, which serves partially for foliage to the street walker, and makes the tree more obvious. Held in the hand the blossoms of some of the elms are quite rich and variegated—now purple and yellowish-specked with the dark anthers etc. and two light styles. I know not why some should be so much earlier than others.

MAY 1, 1852
The flowers (male) of the maple by the bridge are all dried up and its buds are just expanding into leaves—while red maples are in their flowering prime. I find by the leaves that this is probably a white maple.[1]

MAY 1, 1853
Columbine Cliff a place to look for early rue anemones and nemorosas and dandelions. The columbines have been out some days. How ornamental to these dark-colored perpendicular cliffs, nodding from the clefts and shelves!

MAY 1, 1855
The water has gone down very fast and the grass has sprung up. There is a strong fresh-marsh scent wafted from the meadows, much like the salt marshes. We sail with a smart wind from the northeast—yet it is warm enough. Horsemint is seen springing up and for two or three days at the bottom of the river and on shore. . . . There is an unaccountable sweetness as of flowers in the air—a true May Day.

MAY 1, 1856
From the hilltop I look over Wheeler's maple swamp. The maple tops are now I would say a bright brick red. It is the red maple's reign now as the peach and the apple will have theirs. Looking over the swamps a quarter of a mile distant you see dimly defined crescents of bright brick red above and amid a maze of ash-colored branches.

MAY 4, 1858
To go among the willows now and hear the bees hum is equal to going some hundreds of miles southward—toward summer.

rue anemone (*Thalictrum anemonoides=T. thalictroides*)

The cassandra (in full bloom) swarms with *little* bees and amid them is one *bumblebee* which they appear to molest from time to time and afterward I see one flying high overhead at Holden Swamp. . . .

Crossing that first Conantum field I perceive a peculiar fragrance in the air (not the meadow fragrance) like that of vernal flowers or of expanding buds. The ground is covered with the mouse-ear in full bloom and it may be that in part. It is a temperate southwest breeze and this is a scent as of willows (flowers and leafets), bluets, violets, shadbush, mouse-ear, etc., combined—or perhaps the last chiefly. At any rate it is very perceptible.

wild columbine (*Aquilegia canadensis*)

MAY 5, 1852

Saxifrage and crowfoot abundant, though I have found but one violet. The crowfoot has a sweet spring-like fragrance like the dandelion if you have many, but very little of it. A gloss like varnish on its thin petals. It makes a show here in the grass over warm rocks. Saxifrage still less scent.

MAY 5, 1855

The small andromeda has lost its reddish leaves, probably about the time it blossomed, and I can neither get the red cathedral window light looking toward the now westering sun in a most favorable position—nor the *gray* colors in the other direction, but it is all a grayish green.

MAY 5, 1859

Am struck by the beauty of the yellow birches now fairly begun to be in bloom at Yellow Birch or Botrychium Swamp. It is perhaps the handsomest tree or shrub yet in bloom (apparently opened yesterday). Of similar character to the alders and poplar, but larger and of higher color. You see a great tree all hung with long yellow or golden tassels at the end of its slender drooping spray—in clusters at intervals of a few inches or a foot. These are all dangling and incessantly waving in the wind—a great display of lively blossoms (lively both by their color and motion) without a particle of leaf. Yet they are dense enough to reveal the outline of the tree, seen against the bare twigs of itself and other trees. The tassels of this one in bloom are elongated to two or three times the length of those of another not in bloom by its side. These dancing tassels have the effect of the leaves of the tremble [quaking aspen, *Populus tremuloides*]. Those not quite open have a rich dark speckled or braided look almost equally handsome. Golden tassels all trembling in the gentlest breeze—the only signs of life on the trees. A careless observer might not notice them at all. The reawakened springy life of the swamp—the product of its golden veins. These graceful pendants, not in too heavy or dense masses, but thinly dispersed with a noble moderation. Great vegetable chandeliers they stand in the swamp.

MAY 5, 1860

Bluets have *spotted* the fields for two or three days, mingled with the reddish luzula as in Conant's field north of Holden Wood toward the brook.

leatherleaf (cassandra, water andromeda,
Andromeda calyculata = *Chamaedaphne calyculata*)

They fill the air with a *sweet* and *innocent* fragrance at a few rods' distance. . . .

There are some dense beds of houstonia in the yard of the old Conantum house.

Some parts of them show of a distinctly bluer shade two rods off. They are most interesting now before many other flowers are out—the grass high—and they have lost their freshness. I sit down by one dense bed of them to examine them. It is about three feet long and two or more wide. The flowers not only crowd one another but are in several tiers one above another, and completely hide the ground—a mass of white. Counting those in a small place, I find that there are about three thousand flowers in a square foot. They are all turned a little toward the sun and emit a refreshing odor. Here is a lumbering bumblebee probing these tiny flowers. It is a rather ludicrous sight. Of course they will not support him—except a little where they are densest—so he bends them down rapidly (hauling them in with his arms, as it were) one after another, thrusting his beak into the tube of each. It takes him but a moment to dispatch one. It is a singular sight, a bumblebee clambering over a bed of these delicate flowers. There are various other bees about them.

MAY 6, 1852

Sat all day with the window open, for the outer air is the warmest. The balm of Gilead was well blossomed out yesterday, and has been for three or four days probably. . . .

It is pleasant when the road winds along the side of a hill with a thin fringe of wood through which to look into the low land. It furnishes both shade and frame for your pictures, as this Corner road. The first *Anemone nemorosa,* windflower or wood anemone, its petals more slightly tinged with purple than the rue-leaved. . . .

Cowslips show at a distance in the meadow (Miles'). The new butter is white still, but with these *cows' lips* in the grass it will soon be yellow, I trust. This yellowness in the spring derived from the sun affects even the cream in the cow's bag, and flowers in yellow butter at last. Who has not turned pale at the sight of hay butter? These are the cows' lips.

MAY 6, 1855

Near Jenny Dugan's perceive that unaccountable fugacious fragrance as of all flowers, bursting forth in air—not near a meadow—which perhaps

I first perceived on May 1st. It is the general fragrance of the year. I am almost afraid I shall trace it to some particular plant. It surpasses all particular fragrances. I am not sitting near any flower that I can perceive.

MAY 6, 1858

Horticulturalists think that they make flower gardens—though in their thoughts they are barren and flowerless—but to the poet the earth is a flower garden wherever he goes, or thinks.

wood anemone (*Anemone nemorosa=A. quinquefolia*)

MAY 6, 1860

Sit on the steep north bank of White Pond. The *Amelanchier Botryapium* [Eastern or smooth shadbush, *A. canadensis* or *A. laevis*] in flower—now spots the brown sproutland hillside on the southeast side across the pond, very interestingly though it makes but a faint impression of color. I see its pink distinctly a quarter of a mile off. It is seen now in sproutlands half a dozen years old—where the oak leaves have just about all fallen except a few white oaks. (It is in prime about the 8th.) Others are seen directly under the bank on which we sit—on this side, very white against the blue water.

Many at this distance would not notice those shadbush flowers on the hillside—or mistake them for whitish rocks. They are the more interesting for coming thus between the fall of the oak leaves and the expanding of other shrubs and trees. Some of the larger near at hand are very light and elegant masses of white bloom. The white-fingered flower of the sprout-lands.

MAY 7, 1853

A few yellow lily pads are already spread out on the surface—tender reddish leaves, with a still crenate or scalloped border like that of some tin platters on which turnovers are cooked. While the muddy bottom is almost everywhere spotted with the large reddish ruffle-like leaves from the midst of which the flower stems already stand up a foot, aiming toward the light and heat. That long reddish bent grass abounds on the river now. That small kind of pondweed with a whorl of small leaves on the surface and nutlets already in the axils of the very narrow linear leaves is common in the river.

MAY 7, 1854

Flowers, e.g. willow and hazel catkins, are self-registering indicators of *fair* weather. I remember how I waited for the hazel catkins to become relaxed and shed their pollen, but they delayed, till at last there came a pleasanter and warmer day and I took off my greatcoat while surveying in the woods—and then when I went to dinner at noon, hazel catkins in full flower were dangling from the banks by the roadside and yellowed my clothes with their pollen. If man is thankful for the serene and warm day, much more are the flowers.

MAY 8, 1852

Children are digging dandelions by the roadside with a pan and a case-knife.

MAY 8, 1853

At the foot of Annursnack rising from the Jesse Hosmer meadow was surprised by the brilliant pale scarlet flowers of the painted cup, *Castilleja coccinea,* just coming into bloom. Some may have been out a day or two. Methinks this the most high-colored and brilliant flower yet, not excepting the columbine. In color it matches Sophia's cactus blossoms exactly. It is all the more interesting for being a painted leaf and not petal, and its spidery leaves, pinnatifid with linear divisions, increase its strangeness. It is now from three to six inches high rising from the moist base of the hill. It is wonderful what a variety of flowers may grow within the range of a walk and how long some very conspicuous ones may escape the most diligent walker. If you do not chance to visit their localities the right week or fortnight, when their signs are out. . . .

The catkins of the black birch appear more advanced than those of the white birch. They are very large, four inches long, half a dozen gracefully drooping at the ends of the twigs bent down by their weight, conspicuous at a distance in wisps, as if dry leaves left on—very rich golden. The yellow birch is the first I have noticed fully in bloom considerably in advance of the others. Its flowers smell like its bark. Methinks the black and the paper birch next, and then the white, or all nearly together. The leaves of the *papyracea* unfold like a fan and are sticky—how fresh and glossy—and the catkins I gather shed pollen the next morning.

MAY 8, 1854

Lee's Cliff is now a perfect natural rockery for flowers. These gray cliffs and scattered rocks with upright faces below reflect the heat like a hothouse. The ground is whitened with the little white cymes of the saxifrage, now shot up to six or eight inches, and more flower-like dangling scarlet columbines are seen against the gray rocks, and here and there the earth is spotted with yellow crowfoots and a *few* early cinquefoils. . . . To which is to be added the scent of bruised catnip—and the greenness produced by many other forward herbs, and all resounding with the hum of insects. And all this while flowers are rare elsewhere. It is as if you had taken a step suddenly a month forward, or had entered a greenhouse.

MAY 8, 1860

The cinquefoil is closed in a cloudy day—and when the sun shines it is turned toward it.

MAY 9, 1852

The *Viola ovata* is one of the minutest of spring flowers—two leaves and a blossom bud showing the blue close to the earth. What haste to push up and open its lesser azure to the greater above. Such a disproportion of blossom to the leaves. Almost literally a pretty delicate blue flower bursting forth from the scurf of the earth.

scarlet painted-cup (Indian paintbrush, *Castilleja coccinea*)

MAY 9, 1858

A dandelion perfectly gone to seed—a complete globe, a system in itself.

MAY 9, 1860

Fir balsam bloom.

    Sugar maple blossoms are now a tender yellow, in prime say 11th.

    Thousands of dandelions along the meadow by the Mill Brook behind R.W.E.'s in prime say 10th. (By the 18th are much concealed by grass.)

MAY 10, 1852

For some reason I now remember the autumn—the succory [chicory] and the goldenrod. We remember autumn to best advantage in the spring—

paper birch (*Betula papyracea=B. papyrifera*)

the finest aroma of it reaches us then. . . . How closely the flower follows upon if it does not precede the leaf! The leaves are but calyx and escort to the flower. Some beds of clover wave.

MAY 10, 1853
I proceed down the Turnpike. The masses of the golden willow are seen in the distance on either side of the way, twice as high as the road is wide,

sugar maple (*Acer saccharum*)

conspicuous against the distant still half-russet hills and forests, for the green grass hardly yet prevails over the dead stubble, and the woods are but just beginning to gray. The female willow is a shade greener. At this season the traveler passes through a golden gate on causeways where these willows are planted, as if he were approaching the entrance to Fairyland—and there will surely be found the yellow bird, and already from a distance is heard his note, a *tche tche tche—tcha tchar tcha*—ah willow willow. Ah could not he truly arrange for us the difficult family of the willows. Better than Borrer, or Barratt of Middletown! And as he passes between the portals a sweet fragrance is wafted to him—he not only breathes but scents and tastes the air—and he hears the low humming or susurrus of a myriad insects which are feeding on its sweets. It is apparently these that attract the yellow bird. The golden gates of the year, the *May*-gate. The traveler cannot pass out of Concord by the highways in any direction without passing between such portals—graceful, curving, drooping wand-like twigs, on which leaves and blossoms appear together. . . . He is the richest who has most use for nature as raw material of tropes and symbols with which to describe his life. If these gates of golden willows affect me they correspond to the beauty and promise of some experience on which I am entering. . . .

I sit here surrounded by hellebores eighteen inches high or more with handsome regular plaited leaves, regularly arranged around the erect stems, and a multitude of ferns are unrolling themselves. Altogether making the impression of a tropical vegetation.

MAY 11, 1853
The gold-thread up for a day or two, though few flowers compared with buds. Not at once referred to its leaf, so distant on its thread-like peduncle. The water saxifrage also for a day or two in some places, on its tall straight stem rising from its whorl of leaves. Sorrel now fairly out in some places. I will put it under May 8th. A high blueberry by Potter's heater piece.[2] A yellow lily.

MAY 11, 1859
Uvularia perfoliata [perfoliate bellwort] out in rain—say then the 9th. Just after plucking it I perceived what I call the *meadow* fragrance though in the woods—but I afterward found that this flower was *peculiarly* fragrant,

false hellebore (*Veratrum viride*)

and its fragrance like *that*, so it was probably this which I had perceived.
S. [Charles Smith] was reminded of the lily of the valley by it.

MAY 12, 1853
A wild pear in blossom on Ponkawtasset, detected by its uprightness and
no large limbs—but the blossoms being white are not so handsome as the
apple, but are earlier. . . .

I am surprised to find the pedicularis or lousewort—a yellowish one out, on a warm bank, near the meadow edge.

MAY 12, 1857

The *Salix cordata* var. *Torreyana* is distinguished by its naked ovaries more or less red-brown with flesh-colored stigmas, with a distinct slender woody rachis and conspicuous stalks—giving the ament a loose and open appearance.

When I consider how many species of willow have been planted along

goldthread (*Coptis trifolia*)

the railroad causeway within ten years—of which no one knows the history—and not one in Concord beside myself can tell the name of one so that it is quite a discovery to identify a single one in a year, and yet within this period the seeds of all these kinds have been conveyed from some other locality to this, I am reminded how much is going on that man wots not of.

MAY 12, 1858
The early form of the cinquefoil is now apparently in prime—and very pretty spotting the banks with its clear bright yellow.

MAY 12, 1860
The sugar maple blossoms on the Common resound with bees.

wood betony (*Pedicularis canadensis*)

MAY 13, 1854

The sand cherry, judging from what I saw yesterday, will begin to flower today.

MAY 14, 1852

The mayflowers which I plucked today surpass all flowers hitherto in fragrance—peeping up from amid the leaves they perfume the roadside. A strawberry by the meadow side, probably the other species. Anemones now in their prime. The bearberry (*Arbutus Uva-Ursi*) [*Arctostaphylos uva-ursi*] in bloom, a neat bell-like white flower with a reddish tinge and red tips, red contracted rim clear pearly and red, transparent at base.

Most men can be easily transplanted from here to there, for they have

wand willow (*Salix cordata=S. eriocephala*)

so little root—no tap root—or their roots penetrate so little way, that you can thrust a shovel quite under them and take them up roots and all.

MAY 14, 1853
The green buds of yellow lilies are bobbing up and down, already showing more or less yellow—this the most forward sign in the water. The great *scalloped* platters of their leaves have begun and show themselves on the surface and the red round leaves of the white lily—now red above as well as below.

MAY 14, 1855
The beech blossom in house opens say tomorrow in woods—and *probably* will leaf generally by the next day.

MAY 14, 1860
The early sedges even in the meadows have blossomed before you are aware of it—while their tufts and bases are still mainly brown.

MAY 15, 1853
Silvery cinquefoil now open. Its petals perchance show the green between them but the beautiful undersides of the leaves more than make up for it. . . .

The golden willow catkins begin to fall—their prime is past—and buttercups and silvery cinquefoil and the first apple blossoms and waving grass beginning to be tinged with sorrel introduce us to a different season. The huckleberry, *resinosa,* its red flowers are open—in more favorable places several days earlier probably. And the earliest shrub and red and black oaks in warm exposures may be set down today. A red butterfly goes by. Methinks I have seen them before. The painted cup is now abundantly and fully out. Six or eight inches high above its spidery leaves, almost like a red flame, it stands on edge of the hill just rising from the meadow—on the instep of the hill. It tells of July with its fiery color. It promises a heat we have not experienced yet. This is a field which lies nearer to summer. Yellow is the color of spring—red of midsummer. Through pale golden and green we arrive at the yellow of the buttercup—through scarlet to the fiery July red, the red lily. . . . The tall buttercup on the west edge of

American beech (*Fagus ferruginea=F. grandifolia*)

Painted Cup Meadow for a day or two at least, and the fringed polygala as long. This side stone bridge, *Barbarea vulgaris,* or common winter cress, yellow rocket, also as long.

Vernal grass quite common at Willis Spring now. Sarsaparilla flower.

Lousewort flower some time and frostbitten.

I was ready to say that I had seen no more beautiful flower than the dandelion. That has the vernal scent. How many flowers have no peculiar, but only this simple vernal fragrance.

The sessile-leaved bellwort with three or four delicate pale green leaves with reflexed edges on a tender-looking stalk. The single modest-colored flower gracefully drooping, neat, with a fugacious richly-spiced fragrance, facing the ground, the dry leaves, as if unworthy to face the heavens. It is

a beautiful sight, a pleasing discovery, the first of the season—growing in a little straggling company, in damp woods or swamps. When you turn up the drooping flower, its petals make a perfect geometrical figure, a six-pointed star. These faint fugacious fragrances are pleasing. You are not always quite sure that you perceive any. . . . The *Viola ovata* is now very common—but rather indistinct in the grass in both high and low land, in the sod where there is yet but little grass. The earth reflects the heavens in violets.

The whole earth is fragrant as a bouquet held to your nose. . . . Methinks the columbine *here* is more remarkable for growing out of the seams of the rocks than the saxifrage, and perhaps better deserves the latter name. It is now in its prime—ornamental for nature's rockwork. It is a beautiful sight

wild sarsaparilla (*Aralia nudicaulis*)

wild oats (sessile-leaved bellwort,
Uvularia sessilifolia)

blue marsh violet
(*Viola cucullata*)

to see large clusters of splendid scarlet and yellow flowers growing out of a seam in the side of this gray cliff. I observe some very *pale* blue *Viola cucullata* in the meadows. . . .

Here on this causeway is the sweetest fragrance I have perceived this season—blown from the newly flooded meadows. I cannot imagine what there is to produce it. No nosegay can equal it. It is ambrosially, nectareally fine and subtle, for you can see naught but the water with green spires of meadow grass rising above it. Yet no flower from the islands of the blessed could smell sweeter. Yet I shall never know whence it comes. Is it not all water plants combined?

E. Hoar saw the henbit, *Lamium amplexicaule,* a week ago from Mr. Pritchard's garden.

Celandine is out a day or more—and rhodora, trillium, and yellow violets yesterday at least. Horse chestnut today. What handsome long yellow thread-like peduncles to the staminate flowers of the sugar maple. Three inches long, tassel-like, appearing with the leaves.

MAY 16, 1854

Butternut will blossom tomorrow. The great fern by sassafras begins to bloom, probably *Osmunda Claytoniana,* two feet high now. Interrupted fern, its very dark heads, soon surmounted with green.

MAY 17, 1852

The shrub oaks are just beginning to blossom.

MAY 17, 1853

Everything has sensibly advanced during the warm and moist night. . . . The *Cornus florida* [flowering dogwood] is blossoming—will be fairly out today. N.B. Involucre not spread and true flowers not open till about May 20th. The *Polygonatum pubescens* one on the Island has just opened. This is the smaller Solomon's seal. . . . The buckbean is out apparently today—the singularly fuzzy-looking blossom. How inconspicuous its leaves now. The rhodora is peculiar for being like the peach a profusion of pink blossoms on a leafless stem. . . . The trientalis, properly called starflower, is a white star single double or treble. The fringed polygala surprises us in meadows or in low woods as a rarer richer and more delicate color—with a singularly tender or delicate-looking leaf. As you approach midsummer the color of flowers is more intense and fiery. The reddest flower is *the* flower especially. Our blood is not white nor is it yellow nor even blue. The nodding trillium has apparently been out a day or two. Methinks it smells like the lady's slipper.

Returning toward Fair Haven I perceive at Potter's fence the first whiff of that ineffable fragrance from the Wheeler meadow—as it were the promise of strawberries, pineapples, etc. in the aroma of their flowers— so blandly sweet. Aroma that fitly foreruns the summer and the autumn's

henbit (*Lamium amplexicaule*)

small Solomon's seal (*Polygonatum pubescens*)

most delicious fruits. It would certainly restore all such sick as could be conscious of it. The odors of no garden are to be named with it—it is wafted from the garden of Gardens.

MAY 17, 1854
The splendid rhodora now sets the swamps on fire with its masses of rich color. It is *one of the first* flowers to catch the eye at a distance in masses— so naked, unconcealed by its own leaves.

MAY 17, 1856
Yellow columbine well out at Lee's one rod from rock, one rod east of ash.

MAY 17, 1857
I just notice the fertile sweet fern bloom on *tall* plants (and others)— where the sterile catkins are falling off above it. Most plants have none.

Finding the *Linaria Canadensis* [old-field toadflax, *Nuttallanthus canadensis*] yesterday at the Cliffs on a very close search for flowers makes me think that by looking very carefully in the most favored and warmest localities you may find most flowers out some weeks even in advance of the rest of their kind. . . . White ash fully in bloom.

MAY 18, 1857

P.M. — To Bateman's Pond via Yellow Birch Swamp with Pratt.

Pratt says he saw the first rhodora and cultivated pear out yesterday. . . . Judging from the flowering of such of the plants as I notice, this is a backward season. There is a very grand and picturesque old yellow birch in the old cellar northwest the yellow birch swamp. Though this stands out in open land it does not shed its pollen yet and its catkins are not much more

nodding trillium (*Trillium cernuum*)

than half elongated—but it is very beautiful as it is, with its dark yellowish tassels variegated with brown. Yet in the swamp westerly the yellow birches are in full bloom, and many catkins strew the ground.

MAY 18, 1860
The sand cherry flower is about in prime. It grows on all sides of short stems which are either upright or spreading, forming often regular solid cylinders twelve to eighteen inches long and only one and a half inches in diameter, the flowers facing out every way. Of uniform diameter, determined by the length of the peduncles. Pretty wands of white flowers, with leafets intermingled.

MAY 19, 1851
Found the *Arum triphyllum* and the nodding trillium or wake robin in

white ash (*Fraxinus americana*)

sweet-fern (*Comptonia peregrina*)

Conant's Swamp. An ash also in bloom there, and the sassafras quite striking.

　Also the fringed polygala by Conantum wood.

MAY 19, 1858
Looking with my glass into the Gourgas pond hole—and see *three* or *four*
buckbean blossoms.

MAY 20, 1852
All flowers are beautiful. The *Salix alba* [white willow] is about out of
bloom. Pads begin to appear though the river is high over the meadows.
A caterpillar's nest on a wild cherry. Some apple trees in blossom. Most are
just ready to burst forth, the leaves being half-formed. I find the feverbush
in bloom but apparently its blossoms are now stale. I must observe it next

jack-in-the-pulpit (*Arisaema triphyllum*)

sassafras (*Sassafras albidum*)

year. They were fresh perhaps a week ago. Currants in bloom by Conant's Spring—are they natives of America? A lady's slipper well budded and now white. The *Viola ovata* is of a deep purple blue—is darkest and has most of the *red* in it. The *V. pedata* is smooth and pale blue delicately tinged with purple reflections. The *cucullata* is more decidedly blue, slaty blue and darkly striated.

MAY 21, 1853

Land on Island. One of the most beautiful things to me now is the reddish ash, and higher the silvery canopies of half a dozen young white oak leaves over their catkins—thousands of little tents pitched in the air for the May training of the flowers, so many little parasols to their tenderer flowers. . . .

Landed beyond the grapevine bower and cleared out the spring of leaves and sticks and mud and deepened it, making an outlet and it soon ran clear and cold. The cress, which proves to be the rock cress, or herb of St. Barbara, is now luxuriant and in bloom in many places along the river, looking like mustard.

MAY 21, 1856

Chelidonium. *Rubus triflorus* [dwarf raspberry, *R. pubescens*] abundantly out at the Sawmill Brook—how long? . . .

Saw two splendid rose-breasted grosbeaks with females in the young wood in Emerson's lot. . . . The *Polygonatum pubescens* there in shade almost out—perhaps elsewhere already.

At the trough near Turnpike near Hosmer's Spring—the perhaps *Stellaria borealis* [Northern stitchwort, *S. calycantha*] of the 15th.

MAY 22, 1853

The krigia [dwarf dandelion, *K. virginica*] out, a redder more July yellow than the dandelion—also a yellow Bethlehem star and ribwort, and the mountain cranberry still here and there in blossom though for the most part small berries formed.

An abundance of saxifrage going to seed and in their midst two or three looking densely white like the pearly everlasting—round dense white

tall buttercup (*Ranunculus acris*)

heads, apparently an abortion, an abnormal state without stamens, etc., which I cannot find described.

MAY 22, 1854
At Clamshell, the small oblong yellow heads of yellow clover, some days. Tall buttercup a day or two. Dandelions for some time gone to seed. Water saxifrage now well out.

MAY 23, 1853
Today I am surprised by the dark orange yellow of the senecio. At first we had the lighter paler spring yellows of willows (cowslips even—for do they not grow a little darker afterward?), dandelion, cinquefoil, then the darker (methinks it is a little darker than the cowslip) and deeper yellow of the buttercup and then this broad distinction between the buttercup

white oak (*Quercus alba*)

and the krigia and senecio. As the seasons revolve toward July. Every new flower that opens no doubt expresses a new mood of the human mind. Have I any dark or ripe orange yellow thoughts to correspond? The flavor of my thoughts begins to correspond. Lupines now for some days, probably about the 19th. Whiteweed [oxeye daisy, *Chrysanthemum leucanthemum*] will open perhaps tomorrow or next day. For some time dandelions and mouse-ear have been seen gone to seed—autumnal sights. I have not yet seen a *white* oak, and put with it swamp *white* and chestnut, fairly in bloom.

MAY 23, 1854

The barbarea has been open several days. The first yellow dorbug struggling in the river.

MAY 23, 1857

I wade in the swamp for the kalmia [bog laurel, *Kalmia polifolia*] amid the water andromeda and the sphagnum, scratching my legs with the first and sinking deep in the last. The water is now gratefully cool to my legs—so far from being poisoned in the strong water of the swamp. It is a sort of baptism for which I had waited.

MAY 24, 1853

The smooth speedwell is in its prime now, whitening the sides of the back road, above the Swamp Bridge and front of Hubbard's. Its sweet little pansy-like face looks up on all sides. . . .

The wild pink was out day before yesterday.

MAY 24, 1854

To Pedrick's meadow. . . . Surprised to find the *Andromeda Polifolia* in bloom and apparently past its prime—at least a week or more. The caly-

common winter cress
(*Barbarea vulgaris*)

63

culata almost completely done and the high blueberry getting thin. It is in water a foot and a half deep and rises but little above it. The water must have been several inches higher when it began to bloom. A timid botanist would never pluck it. Its flowers are more interesting than any of its family, almost globular — crystalline white even the calyx except its tips tinged with red or rose. Properly called water andromeda: you must wade into water a foot or two deep to get it.

MAY 24, 1855
Black oak pollen yesterday at least. *Scarlet* oak the same but a little later. The staminate flowers of the first are on long and handsome tassels — for

bog-rosemary (*Andromeda polifolia*)

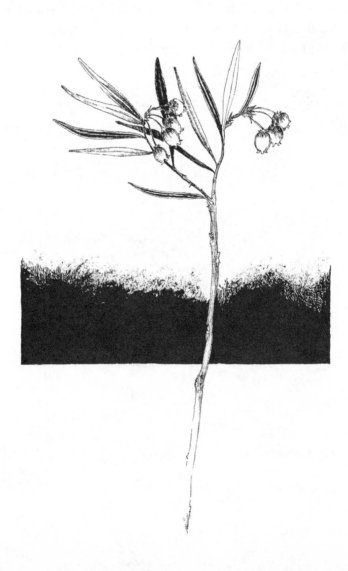

buckbean (*Menyanthes trifoliata*)

three or four inches along the extremities of last year's shoots depending
five inches (sometimes six) by four in width and quite dense and thick.
The scarlet oak tassels are hardly half as long. The leaves much greener and
smoother—and now somewhat wilted emit a sweet odor which those of
the black do not. Both these oaks are apparently more forward at top—
where I cannot see them. . . .

Andromeda Polifolia now in prime—but the leaves are apt to be blackened and unsightly, and the flowers though delicate have a feeble and sickly look, rose white—somewhat crystalline. Its shoots or new leaves unfolding say when it flowered or directly after now one inch long. Buckbean just *fairly* begun, though probably first the 18th—a handsome flower but already when the raceme is only half blown some of the lowest flowers are brown and withered, deforming it. What a pity!

MAY 24, 1857
White ash apparently yesterday at Grape Shore—but not at Conantum. What a singular appearance for some weeks its great masses of dark purple anthers have made—fruit-like on the trees!

MAY 25, 1851
Noticed what I think must be a young poison sumac abundant by the roadside in woods, with last year's berries—with small greenish yellow flowers but leaves not pinnatifid three together. From one to two feet high. What is it?[3]

What is the orange yellow aster-like flower of the meadows now in blossom with a sweet smelling stem when bruised?

What the delicate pinkish and yellowish flower with hoary green stems and leaves of rocky hills?

MAY 25, 1853
The hedge mustard is just out.

MAY 25, 1857
The black spruce of Holden's apparently yesterday but not the 23d.

What a glorious crimson fire as you look up at the sunlight through the thin edges of the scales of its cones!—so intensely glowing in their cool green beds!—while their purplish sterile blossoms shed pollen on you. Took up four young spruce and brought them home in the boat.

After all, I seem to have distinguished only one spruce and that the black, judging by the cones.[4] Perhaps the dark and light varieties of it—for the last is said to be very like the white spruce. The white spruce cones are cylindrical and have an entire firm edge to the scales and the needles are longer.

hedge-mustard (*Sisymbrium officinale*)

MAY 26, 1852

Walking home from surveying. — The fields are *just beginning* to be reddened with sorrel. . . . Channing says he has seen a red clover blossom — and heard a stake-driver. Lousewort, *Pedicularis Canadensis,* very badly named.

MAY 26, 1853

That barberry bush near the bars on Conantum is methinks now the most beautiful, light, and graceful bush that I ever saw in bloom. It is shaped like a haycock, broad and dense, yet light as if some leaven had raised it. But how orientally beautiful now seen through this dark mizzling air, its parallel or rather concentric wreaths composed of leaves and flowers keeping each other apart and lightening the whole mass — each wreath above composed of rich dark green leaves, below of drooping racemes of lively yellow flowers. Its beauty consists in a great measure in this intimate mixture of flowers and leaves — the small rich-colored flowers not being too much massed. It suggests the yellow-robed priests perchance of Thibet (?). The lowest wreaths lie on the ground. But go not so near as to be disturbed by that sickening buttery odor — as of an underdone butter pudding, with too many eggs and too little seasoning in it. Who would think this would bake into such a red acid fruit?

MAY 26, 1855

White oak pollen. The oaks apparently shed pollen about four days later than last year — May be owing to the recent cold weather.

MAY 26, 1859

The rhodora at Ledum Swamp is now in its perfection — brilliant islands of color.

MAY 27, 1852

A wet day. The veery sings nevertheless. The road is white with the apple blossoms fallen off as with snowflakes. The dogwood is coming out. Lady's slippers out. They perfume the air. . . . The nodding trillium has a faint

Canada mayflower (twisted-stalk, wild lily-of-the-valley, *Convallaria bifolia=Maianthemum canadense*)

rich scent. The *Convallaria bifolia* a strong but not very pleasant scent. . . .
The smooth speedwell, the minute pale blue striated flower by the roadsides and in the short sod of fields common now. . . . The fringed polygala
near the Corner Spring is a delicate flower, with very fresh tender green
leaves and red-purple blossoms—beautiful from the contrast of its clear
red-purple flowers with its clear green leaves.

MAY 27, 1853

The *Cornus florida* now fairly out and the involucres are now not greenish white but white tipped with reddish—like a small flock of white birds
passing. Three and a half inches in diameter the larger ones as I find by
measuring. It is something quite novel in the tree line. . . . How beautiful the geranium flower buds just opening, little purple cylindrical tubes
or hoods—cigaritos—with the petals lapped over and round each other.
One opens visibly in a pitcher before me. . . . Yellow clover is out—how

long? Hellebore a day or two at Sawmill Brook, its great spike of green flowers with yellow anthers. Its great plaited leaves look like a green shirt bosom—drawn out smooth they prove to be basins.

MAY 27, 1857
Some butternut catkins—the leaves have been touched by frost. This is blossom week, beginning last Sunday (the 24th).

fringed polygala (*Polygala paucifolia*)

wild geranium (*Geranium maculatum*)

MAY 28, 1853

The bulbous arethusa out a day or two, probably yesterday. Though in a measure prepared for it, still its beauty surprised me—it is by far the highest and richest color yet. Its intense color in the midst of the green meadow made it look twice as large as reality. It looks very foreign in the midst of our plants—its richly freckled, curled, and bearded lip.

MAY 28, 1854

The huckleberries, excepting the late, are now generally in blossom, their rich clear red contrasting with the light green leaves—frequented by honeybees, full of promise for the summer. One of the great crops of the year.

butternut (*Juglans cinerea*)

Thimbleberry two or three days. Cattle stand in the river by the bridge for coolness. Place my hat lightly on my head that the air may circulate beneath. Wild roses budded before you know it—will be out often before you know they are budded. Fields are whitened with mouse-ear gone to seed—a mass of white fuzz blowing off one side—and also with dandelion globes of seeds. Some plants have already reached their fall.

tall meadow-rue (*Thalictrum cornuti=T. pubescens*)

MAY 29, 1854

The chokecherry is leaving off to bloom now that the black cherry is beginning.

MAY 29, 1856

To return to Painted Cup Meadow—I do not perceive the rank odor of *Thalictrum Cornuti* expanding leaves today. How more than fugacious it is! Evidently this odor is emitted only at particular times. A cuckoo's note—loud and hollow from a woodside. Found a painted cup with more yellow than usual in it—and at length Edith found one perfectly yellow. What a flowery place, a vale of Enna, is that meadow.

MAY 29, 1857

I sit at my ease and look out from under my lichen-clad rocky roof—halfway up the Cliff—under freshly leafing ash and hickory trees onto the pond, while the rain is falling faster and faster, and I am rather glad of the rain which affords me this experience. . . . I perceive the buttery-like scent of barberry bloom from over the rock—and now and for some days the bunches of effete white ash anthers strew the ground.

MAY 30, 1852

Now is the summer come. A breezy washing day. A day for shadows—even of moving clouds—over the fields in which the grass is beginning to wave. Senecio in bloom. A bird's nest in grass with coffee-colored eggs. Cinquefoil and houstonia cover the ground, mixed with the grass and contrasting with each other. Strong light, and shades now. Wild cherry on the low shrubs but not yet the trees—a rummy scent. Violets everywhere spot the meadows—some more purple, some more lilac. . . . The *Drosera rotundifolia* now glistens with its dew at midday, a beautiful object closely examined. . . . The anemones appear to be nearly gone. Yellow lilies are abundant. The bulbous arethusa, the most splendid rich and high-colored flower thus far methinks, all flower and color—almost without leaves, and looking much larger than it is and more conspicuous on account of its intense color. A flower of mark. . . . The sumac (*glabra*) is well under way now. The yellow water ranunculus by the Corner causeway.

MAY 30, 1853

Young bush-like black cherries a day or two on Cliffs and in such favorable

places. . . . Landed at a high lupine bank by Carlisle Bridge. How many such lupine banks there are! Whose blue you detect many rods off. There I found methinks minute *specularia* perfoliatas, with small crenate clasping leaves alternate at some distance apart on upright stems, about three inches high, but apparently *fruiting in the bud*.

MAY 30, 1854

I am surprised to find arethusas abundantly out in Hubbard's Close maybe two or three days, though not yet at Arethusa Meadow, probably on account of the recent freshet. It is so leafless that it shoots up unexpectedly. It is all color, a little hook of purple flame projecting from the meadow into the air. Some are comparatively pale. This high-colored plant shoots up suddenly, all flower, in meadows where it is wet walking. A superb flower. . . .

The pink is certainly one of the finest of our flowers, and deserves the

round-leaved sundew (*Drosera rotundifolia*)

place it holds in my memory. It is now in its prime on the south side of the Heywood Peak, where it grows luxuriantly in dense rounded tufts or hemispheres, raying out on every side and presenting an even and regular surface of expanded flowers. I count in one such tuft of an oval form twelve inches by eight some three hundred fully open and about three times as many buds—more than a thousand in all. Some tufts consist wholly of white ones with a very faint tinge of pink.

MAY 30, 1855

Buttonwood flowers now effete—fertile flowers were not brown on the 24th but were the 28th. Say then about the 26th. . . .

The myrica bayberry plucked on the 23d—now first sheds pollen in house, the leaf being but little more expanded on the flowering shoot. Gray says "somewhat preceding the flowers." The catkins about a quarter of an inch long, erect, sterile—oval on the sides of last year's twigs.

Venus'-looking-glass
(*Specularia perfoliata=Triodanis perfoliata*)

MAY 30, 1856

The lady's slipper in pitch pine woodside near J. Hosmer's Desert, probably about the 27th.

MAY 30, 1857

Buttercups thickly spot the churchyard.

MAY 30, 1858

Ledum, one flower out, but perhaps if Pratt had not plucked some last Sunday it might have bloomed here yesterday? It is decidedly leafing also.

MAY 31, 1850

The blossoms of the tough and vivacious shrub oak are very handsome.

northern bayberry (*Myrica pensylvanica*)

MAY 31, 1853

Some incidents in my life have seemed far more allegorical than actual—
they were so significant that they plainly served no other use. That is, I
have been more impressed by their allegorical significance and fitness—
they have been like myths or passages in a myth, rather than mere incidents or history which have to wait to become significant. Quite in harmony with my subjective philosophy. This for instance—that when I
thought I knew the flowers so well, the beautiful purple azalea or pinxter
flower should be shown me by the hunter who found it. . . . The fact that
a rare and beautiful flower which we never saw—perhaps never heard [of],
for which therefore there was no place in our thoughts, may at length be
found in our immediate neighborhood, is very suggestive. . . .

I am going in search of the *Azalea nudiflora*. (Sophia brought home a
single flower without twig or leaf from Mrs. Brooks' last evening.) Mrs.
Brooks I find has a large twig in a vase of water—still pretty fresh, which
she says George Melvin gave to her son George. I called at his office. He
says that Melvin came in to Mr. Gourgas' office where he and others were

pink lady's-slipper (moccasin flower, *Cypripedium acaule*)

sitting Saturday evening with his arms full and gave each a sprig, but he doesn't know where he got it. Somebody, I heard, had seen it at Captain Jarvis' so I went there. I found that they had some still pretty fresh in the house. Melvin gave it to them Saturday night—but they did not know where he got it. A young man working at Stedman Buttrick's said it was a secret. There was only one bush in the town. Melvin knew of it and Stedman knew. When asked Melvin said he got it in the swamp—or from a bush, etc. The young man thought it grew on the Island across the river on the Wheeler Farm. I went on to Melvin's house, though I did not expect to find him at home at this hour, so early in the afternoon. (Saw the woodsorrel out, a day or two perhaps by the way.) At length I saw his dog by the door and knew he was at home.

He was sitting in the shade bareheaded at his back door. He had a large pailful of the azalea recently plucked—in the shade behind his house, which he said he was going to carry to town at evening. He had also a sprig set out. He had been out all the forenoon and said he had got seven pickerel—perhaps—apparently he had been drinking and was just getting over it. At first he was a little sly about telling me where the azalea grew, but I saw that I should get it out of him. He dilly-dallied a little— called to his neighbor Farmer whom he called Razor to know if he could tell me where that flower grew. He called it by the way the "red honeysuckle." This was to prolong the time and make the most of his secret. I felt pretty sure the plant was to be found on Wheeler's land beyond the river, as the young man had said. For I had remembered how some weeks before this when I went up the Assabet after the yellow rocket, I saw Melvin who had just crossed with his dog, and when I landed to pluck the rocket he appeared out of the woods, said he was after a fish pole and asked me the name of my flower. Didn't think it was very handsome— "not so handsome as the honeysuckle is it?" And now I knew it was his "red honeysuckle" and not the columbine he meant. Well, I told him he had better tell me where it was—I was a botanist and ought to know. But he thought I couldn't possibly find it by his directions. I told him he'd better tell me and have the glory of it, for I should surely find it if he didn't. I'd got a clue to it and shouldn't give it up. I should go over the river for it. I could smell it a good way, you know. He thought I could smell it half a mile—and he wondered however that I hadn't stumbled on it, or Channing. Channing he said came close by it once—when it was in flower. He thought he'd surely find it then—but he didn't, and he said nothing to him.

He told me he found it about ten years ago—and he went to it every year. It blossomed at the old election time, and he thought it "the handsomest flower that grows." . . .

We went on down the brook—Melvin and I and his dog—and crossed the river in his boat, and he conducted me to where the *Azalea nudiflora* grew—it was a little past its prime, perhaps—and showed me how near Channing came. ("You won't tell him what I said, will you?" said he.) I offered to pay him for his trouble but he wouldn't take anything. He had just as lief I'd know as not. He thought it first came out last Wednesday, on the 25th. . . . It is a conspicuously beautiful flowering shrub—with the sweet fragrance of the common swamp pink but the flowers are larger and in this case a fine lively rosy pink, not so clammy as the other.

JUNE 2, 1852
Golden alexanders—looks like a parsnip—near or beyond the East Quarter schoolhouse. The barberry blossoms are now abundant. They fill the air with a disagreeable buttery fragrance. Low blackberry in bloom.

JUNE 2, 1853
Clintonia borealis a day or two.

This is perhaps the most interesting and neatest of what I may call the liliaceous (?) plants we have. Its beauty at present consists chiefly in its commonly three very handsome rich clear dark green leaves—which Bigelow describes truly as "more than half a foot long, oblanceolate, smooth and shining." They are perfect in form and color, broadly oblanceolate with a deep channel down the middle, uninjured by insects—arching over from a center at the ground sometimes very symmetrically disposed in a triangular fashion, and from their midst rises the scape a foot high with one or more umbels of "green bell-shaped flowers": yellowish green nodding or bent downward but without fragrance. In fact the flower is all green both leaves and corolla. The leaves alone—and many have no scape—would detain the walker. Its berries are its flower. A single plant is a great ornament in a vase—from the beauty of its form and the rich unspotted green of its leaves.

The sorrel now reddens the fields far and wide. . . . The medeola has

golden alexanders (*Zizia aurea*)

been out a day or two apparently, another green flower. . . . The pinxter flower growing as it does in an underwood in the shade of larger trees — the naked umbels of its lively rose pink flowers are seen flashing out against a background of green or of dark shaded recesses. The lobes of the corolla are of a lively rose pink, the tubes and stamens of a deeper red.

JUNE 2, 1854
The rue just budded smells remarkably like a skunk and also like a rank dog. Strange affinity!

JUNE 2, 1860
Red clover first seen. . . .
    The yellow Bethlehem star is pretty common now.

The painted cup is in its prime. It reddens the meadow—Painted Cup Meadow. It is a splendid show of brilliant scarlet—the color of the cardinal flower and surpassing it in *mass* and *profusion.* They first appear on the side of the hill in drier ground, half a dozen inches high, and their color is most striking then when it is most rare and precious, but they now cover the meadow mingled with buttercups, etc., and many are more than eighteen inches high. I do not like the name—it does not remind me of a cup, rather of a flame when it first appears. It might be called flame flower, or scarlet tip. Here is a large meadow full of it and yet very few in the town have ever seen it.

yellow clintonia (*Clintonia borealis*)

common stargrass (*Hypoxis erecta=H. hirsuta*)

JUNE 3, 1857

The ground of the cedar swamp where it has been burnt over and sprouts, etc., have sprung up again is covered with the *Marchantia poly-morpha* [common liverwort]. Now shows its starlike or umbrella-shaped fertile flowers and its shield-shaped sterile ones. It is a very rank and wild-looking vegetation forming the cuticle of the swamp's foundation.

JUNE 4, 1852

The golden alexanders is called *Zizia aurea*. The cistus is out. Lupines in prime. The Canada snapdragon, that little blue flower that lasts so long, grows with the lupines under Fair Haven. The early chickweed with the star-shaped flower is common in fields now.

white baneberry (*Actaea alba=A. pachypoda*)

JUNE 4, 1853

The vetch just out by Turnpike—dark-violet purple.

JUNE 4, 1855

Ellen Emerson finds the *Viola pubescens* [downy yellow violet] scarce today—but the *Actaea alba* in full bloom.

JUNE 5, 1852

The lupine is now in its glory. It is the more important because it occurs in such extensive patches, even an acre or more together, and of such a pleasing variety of colors, purple, pink, or lilac—and white, especially with the sun on it, when the transparency of the flower makes its color changeable. It paints a whole hillside with its blue, making such a field (if not meadow) as Proserpine might have wandered in. Its leaf was made to be covered with

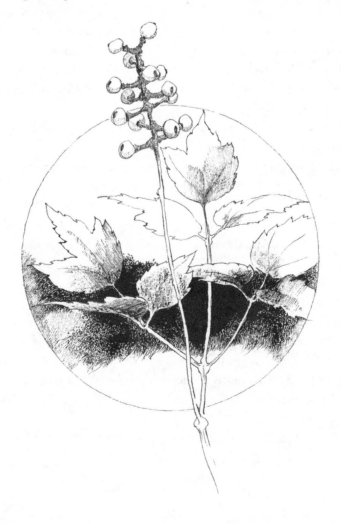

dewdrops. I am quite excited by this prospect of blue flowers in clumps with narrow intervals. Such a profusion of the heavenly, the elysian color, as if these were the Elysian Fields. They say the seeds look like babies' faces and hence the flower is so named. No other flowers exhibit so much blue. That is the value of the lupine. The earth is blued with them. Yet a third of a mile distant I do not detect their color on the hillside. Perchance because it is the color of the air.

JUNE 5, 1856

Everywhere now in dry pitch pine woods stand the red lady's slippers over the red pine leaves on the forest floor—rejoicing in June with their two broad curving green leaves (some even in swamps). Uphold their rich striped red drooping sack. This while rye begins to wave richly in the fields.

JUNE 5, 1857

I am interested in each contemporary plant in my vicinity—and have attained to a certain acquaintance with the larger ones. They are cohabitants with me of this part of the planet, and they bear familiar names. Yet how essentially wild they are—as wild really as those strange fossil plants whose impressions I see on my coal.

JUNE 6, 1851

Gathered tonight the *Cicuta maculata,* American hemlock, the veins of the leafets ending in the notches and the root fasciculated.

JUNE 6, 1852

The side-flowering sandwort, an inconspicuous white flower like a chick-weed.

JUNE 6, 1856

That willow male and female opposite to Trillium Woods on the railroad I find to be the *Salix rostrata* or long-beaked willow—one of the *ochre-flowered* (*fulvae*) willows of Barratt. It is now just *beginning* to open its long beaks. The *S. cordata* is another of the ochre-flowered ones.

JUNE 6, 1857

Krigias, with their somewhat orange yellow, spot the dry hills all the forenoon and are very common but as they are closed in the afternoon they are but rarely noticed by walkers.

JUNE 6, 1858
Am surprised to find that the buckbean flowers are withered, being killed by the recent frosts. Yellow Bethlehem star.

JUNE 7, 1854
Along the woodpaths and in woodside pastures I see the golden basins of the cistus. I am surprised at the size of green berries—shadbush, low blueberries, chokecherries, etc., etc. It is but a step from flowers to fruit.

JUNE 7, 1857
Sunday. P.M. to river and Ponkawtasset with M. Pratt. . . .

cowbane
(American hemlock, *Cicuta maculata*)

wild calla (*Calla palustris*)

Pratt has got the *Calla palustris* in prime—some was withering so it may have been out ten days—from the bog near Bateman's Pond. Also *Oxalis violacea* [violet wood-sorrel] which he says began about last Sunday or May 31st. Larger and handsomer than the yellow, though it blossoms but sparingly.

JUNE 7, 1860
White clover already whitens some fields and resounds with bees.

JUNE 8, 1853
White pine in flower—all the female flowers on the very tops of the trees, a small crimson cone upright on the ends of its peduncles, while the last year's now three or four inches long and green are curved downward like scythes. Best seen looking down on the tops of lower pines from the top of a higher one. Apparently just beginning.[5]

The early potentilla is now in some places erect. The sidesaddle flower is out how long? And the sweet flag how long?

I see the pollen of the pitch pine now beginning to cover the surface of the pond. Most of the pines at the north-northwest end have none, and on some there is only one pollen-bearing flower.

The yellow water ranunculus is an important flower in the river now, rising above the white lily pads whose flower does not yet appear. I perceive that their petals washed ashore line the sand conspicuously.

pitcher plant (*Sarracenia purpurea*)

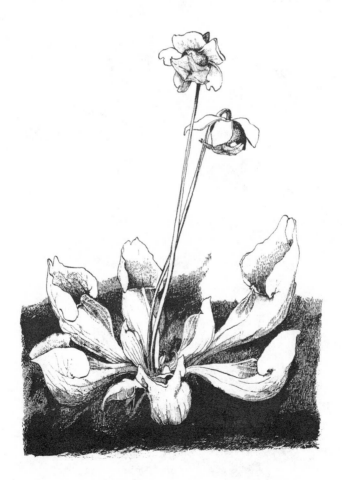

JUNE 9, 1853

The steam of the engine streaming far behind is regularly divided as if it were the vertebrae of a serpent—probably by the strokes of the piston. The reddish seeds or glumes of grasses cover my boots now in the dewy or foggy morning. The diervilla out apparently yesterday. The first white lily bud. White clover is abundant and very sweet on the common, filling the air—but not yet elsewhere as last year. . . .

Hear a goldfinch—this the second or third only that I have heard. Whiteweed now whitens the fields. There are many *star* flowers. I remember the anemone especially the rue anemone which is not yet all gone lasting longer than the true one—above all the trientalis, and of late the yellow Bethlehem star, and perhaps others. . . . The meadows are now yellow with the golden senecio, a more orange yellow—mingled with the light glossy yellow of the buttercup.

starflower (*Trientalis americana* = *T. borealis*)

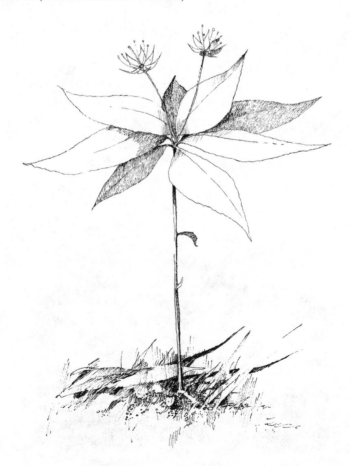

tufted rush (*Juncus effusus*)

JUNE 9, 1854

Find the great fringed orchis out apparently two or three days. Two are almost fully out, two or three only budded. A large spike of peculiarly delicate pale purple flowers growing in the luxuriant and shady swamp amid hellebores, ferns, golden senecios, etc., etc. It is remarkable that this, one of the fairest of all our flowers, should also be one of the rarest—for the most part not seen at all. I think that no other but myself in Concord annually finds it.

JUNE 9, 1858

High blackberry not long. I notice by the roadside at Moore's Swamp the very common *Juncus effusus*—not quite out—one to two and a half feet high.

JUNE 10, 1852

The maple-leaved viburnum at Laurel Glen. Also the round-leaved cornel. The mountain laurel is budded.[6] The yellow diervilla (*D. trifida*) [bush-

honeysuckle, *D. lonicera*] ready to blossom there. . . . I perceived that untraceable odor by the shore of Walden near railroad where there are grapevines—and yet the vines do not smell and I have perceived it for two or three weeks. The vines appear but just in flower. Bittersweet woody nightshade, *Solanum Dulcamara*. It has a singular strong odor. . . .

The pyrolas now ready to blossom. Shinleaf is a good name for one. . . . *Utricularia vulgaris,* common bladderwort, a dirty conditioned flower like a sluttish woman with a gaudy yellow bonnet. Is the grape out? Solomon's seal two-leaved with a third? *Sanicula Marylandica* (black snakeroot) without color at first glance like a buttercup, leaf and stem.

shinleaf (*Pyrola elliptica*)

JUNE 10, 1853

What shall this great wild tract over which we strolled be called? . . . The old Carlisle road which runs through the middle of it is bordered on each side with wild apple pastures—where the trees stand without order having many if not most of them sprung up by accident or from pomace sown at random and are for the most part concealed by birches and pines. These orchards are very extensive and yet many of these apple trees growing as forest trees bear good crops of apples. It is a paradise for walkers in the fall. There are also boundless huckleberry pastures as well as many blueberry swamps. Shall we call it the Easterbrooks Country? . . .

High blackberries conspicuously in bloom whitening the sides of lanes.

JUNE 11, 1851

The woodland paths are never seen to such advantage as in a moonlight night so embowered—still opening before you almost against expectation as you walk. You are so completely in the woods and yet your feet meet no obstacles. It is as if it were not a path but an open winding passage through the bushes which your feet find. . . .

black snakeroot (*Sanicula marilandica*)

By night no flowers, at least no variety of colors. The pinks are no longer pink—they only shine faintly, reflecting more light. Instead of flowers underfoot, stars overhead.

The meadows are yellow with golden senecio. Marsh speedwell, *Veronica scutellata,* lilac-tinted, rather pretty. The mouse-ear forget-me-not *Myosotis laxa* has now extended its racemes (?) very much and hangs over the edge of the brook. It is one of the most interesting minute flowers. It is the more beautiful for being small and unpretending—for even flowers must be modest. . . . Some fields are now almost wholly covered with sheep's sorrel, now turned red—its valves (?). It helps thus agreeably to paint the earth—contrasting even at a distance with the greener fields, blue sky, and dark or downy clouds. It is red marbled watered mottled or waved with greenish—like waving grain, three or four acres of it. To the farmer or grazier it is a troublesome weed—but to the landscape viewer an agreeable red tinge laid on by the painter. I feel well into summer when I see this redness. It appears to be avoided by the cows.

The locust in graveyard shows but few blossoms yet. It is very hot this afternoon, and that peculiar stillness of summer noons now reigns in the woods.

The *Carex tentaculata* [sallow sedge, *C. lurida*] at Clamshell in prime (say a week). It *abounds* at Forget-me-not Shore—dense-flowered spreading spikes.

Maple-leaved viburnum well out at Laurel Glen probably 9th. The laurel probably by day after tomorrow. The note of the wood thrush answers to some cool unexhausted morning vigor in the hearer. The leaf of the rattlesnake plantain now surprises the walker amid the dry leaves on cool hillsides in the woods. Of very simple form but richly veined with longitudinal and transverse white veins. It looks like art. . . .

Visited the great orchis which I am waiting to have open completely. It

sallow sedge (*Carex tentaculata=C. lurida*)

is emphatically a flower (within gunshot of the hawk's nest), its great spike six inches by two of delicate pale purple flowers which begin to expand at bottom, rises above and contrasts with the green leaves of the hellebore and skunk cabbage and ferns (by which its own leaves are concealed) in the cool shade of an alder swamp. . . .

Norway cinquefoil. A wild moss rose in Arethusa Meadow, where are arethusas lingering still.

JUNE 13, 1852
Lambkill is out. I remember with what delight I used to discover this

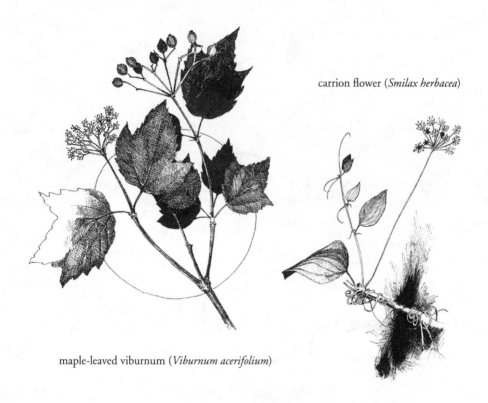

carrion flower (*Smilax herbacea*)

maple-leaved viburnum (*Viburnum acerifolium*)

flower in dewy mornings. All things in this world must be seen with the morning dew on them. Must be seen with youthful early-opened hopeful eyes. . . . The *Smilax herbacea,* carrion flower, a rank green vine with long-peduncled umbels, with small greenish or yellowish flowers just opening, and tendrils, at the Miles swamp. It smells exactly like a dead rat in the wall—and apparently attracts flies (I find small gnats on it) like carrion. A very remarkable odor—a single minute flower in an umbel open will scent a whole room. Nature imitates all things in flowers. They are at once the most beautiful and the ugliest objects—the most fragrant and the most offensive to the nostrils, etc., etc. . . .

Orobanche uniflora, single-flowered broomrape (Bigelow), [or] *Aphyllon uniflorum,* one-flowered cancer root (Gray). C. found it June 12 at Clematis Brook.

JUNE 13, 1853

Violets appear to be about done generally. Four-leaved loosestrife just out, also the smooth wild rose yesterday. The pogonia at Forget-me-not Brook.

How beautiful the solid cylinders of the lambkill now just before sunset, small ten-sided rosy-crimson basins, about two inches above the recurved drooping dry capsules of last year—and sometimes those of the year before are two inches lower. The first rose bug on one of these flowers.

The ledum has grown three or four inches (as well as the andromeda). It has a rather agreeable fragrance—between turpentine and strawberries. It is rather strong and penetrating and sometimes reminds me of the peculiar scent of a bee. The young leaves bruised and touched to the nose even make it smart. It is the young and expanding ledum leaves which are so fragrant.

one-flowered cancer root (*Orobanche uniflora*)

JUNE 14, 1860

The white water ranunculus is abundant in the brook—out say a week, and *well open in the sunshine.* It is [a] pretty white flower (with yellow center) seen above the dark brown green leaves in the rapid water, its peduncle recurved so as to present the flower erect half an inch to an inch above the surface—while the buds are submerged.

JUNE 15, 1851

Saw the first wild rose today on the west side of the railroad causeway. The whiteweed has suddenly appeared and the clover gives whole fields a rich and florid appearance. The rich red and the sweet scented white. The fields are blushing with the red species as the western sky at evening. . . .

I see the tall crowfoot now in the meadows—*Ranunculus acris*—with a smooth stem. I do not notice the *bulbosus* [bulbous buttercup, *R. bulbosus*] which was so common a fortnight ago. The rose-colored flowers of the *Kalmia angustifolia,* lambkill, just opened and opening. The *Convallaria bifolia* growing stale in the woods. The *Hieracium venosum,* veiny-leaved hawkweed [rattlesnake weed], with its yellow blossoms in the woodland path. The *Hypoxis erecta,* yellow Bethlehem star where there is a thick wiry grass in open paths should be called yellow-eyed grass methinks. The *Pyrola asarifolia* [green pyrola, *P. chlorantha*] with its pagoda-like stem of flowers i.e. broad-leaved wintergreen. The *Trientalis Americana* like last in the woods—with its star-like white flower and pointed whorled leaves. The prunella too is in blossom and the rather delicate *Thesium umbellatum,* a white flower.

JUNE 15, 1852

How rapidly new flowers unfold—as if nature would get through her work too soon. One has as much as he can do to observe how flowers successively unfold. It is a flowery revolution to which but few attend. Hardly too much attention can be bestowed on flowers. We follow, we march after, the highest color—that is our flag, our standard, our "color." Flowers were made to be seen, not overlooked. Their bright colors imply eyes, spectators. There have been many flower men who have rambled the world over to see them. The flowers robbed from an Egyptian traveler were at length carefully boxed up and forwarded to Linnaeus, the man of flowers. . . . The maple-leaved viburnum is opening with a purplish tinge. . . .

Here also, at Well Meadow Head, I see the fringed purple orchis—
unexpectedly beautiful, though a pale lilac purple—a large spike of purple
flowers. . . . I am not prepared to say it is the most beautiful wildflower
I have found this year. Why does it grow there only—far in a swamp remote from public view? It is somewhat fragrant, reminding me of the
lady's slipper.

heal-all (*Prunella vulgaris*)

bastard toadflax (*Thesium umbellatum=Comandra umbellata*)

Clover now in its prime. What more luxuriant than a clover field? The poorest soil that is covered with it looks incomparably fertile. This is perhaps the most characteristic feature of June, resounding with the hum of insects. . . . The rude health of the sorrel cheek has given place to the blush of clover. Painters are wont in their pictures of paradise to strew the ground too thickly with flowers. There should be moderation in all things. Though we love flowers we do not want them so thick under our feet that we cannot walk without treading on them. But a clover field in bloom is some excuse for them. . . .

Here are many wild roses northeast of Trillium Woods. We are liable to underrate this flower on account of its commonness. Is it not the queen of our flowers? How ample and high-colored its petals, glancing half concealed from its own green bowers. There is a certain noble and delicate civility about it, not wildness. . . . I bring home the buds ready to expand, put them in a pitcher of water and the next morning they open and fill my chamber with fragrance. This found in the wilderness must have reminded the Pilgrim of home.

Observed yesterday the erigeron with a purple tinge. I cannot tell whether this which seems in other respects the same with the white is the *strigosus* or *annuus*. . . . Again I scent the white water lily and a season I had waited for is arrived. How indispensable all these experiences to make up the summer. It is the emblem of purity, and its scent suggests it. Growing in stagnant and muddy [water] it bursts up so pure and fair to the eye and so sweet to the scent—as if to show us what purity and sweetness reside in and can be extracted from the slime and muck of earth. I think I have plucked the first one that has opened for a mile at least. What confirmation of our hopes is in the fragrance of the water lily. I shall not so soon despair of the world for it notwithstanding slavery—and the cowardice and want of principle of the North. It suggests that the time may come when man's deeds will smell as sweet. Such then is the odor our planet emits. . . .

The *Rosa nitida* [shining rose] grows along the edge of the ditches—the half-open flowers showing the deepest rosy tints. So glowing that they make an evening or twilight of the surrounding afternoon, seeming to stand in the shade or twilight. Already the bright petals of yesterday's flowers are thickly strewn along on the black mud at the bottom of the ditch.

The *R. nitida* the earlier (?) with its narrow shiny leaves and prickly stem and its moderate-sized rose-pink petals.

The *R. lucida* with its broader and duller leaves but larger and perhaps deeper-colored and more purple petals—perhaps yet higher scented—and its great yellow center of stamens. . . .

It is eight days since I plucked the great orchis—one is perfectly fresh still in my pitcher. It may be plucked when the spike is only half opened and will open completely and keep perfectly fresh in a pitcher more than a week. Do I not live in a garden—in paradise? I can go out each morning before breakfast—and do—and gather these flowers, with which to perfume my chamber where I read and write, all day.

JUNE 16, 1858
How agreeable and wholesome the fragrance of the low blackberry blossom—reminding me of all the rosaceous fruit-bearing plants, so near and

Carolina rose
(*Rosa carolina*)

dear to our humanity. It is one of the most deliciously fragrant flowers, reminding of wholesome fruits.

JUNE 17, 1853
The pogonias, adder's tongue arethusas, I see nowadays, getting to be numerous, are far too pale to compete with the *A. bulbosa,* and then their snake-like odor is much against them.

JUNE 17, 1854
Morning glory apparently yesterday. Well named morning glory. Its broad bell- and trumpet-shaped flowers faintly tinged with red are like the dawn itself. The new pitcher plant leaf is formed in some places, now free from insects. Pogonia *perhaps* a day or two.

JUNE 19, 1852
The orchis keeps well. One put in my hat this morning and carried all day will last fresh a day or two at home. These are peculiar days when you find the purple orchis and the arethusas too in the meadows.

JUNE 19, 1860
Some tall rough goldenrod is three feet high and generally in rich ground it is two or more. Also some fragrant goldenrod is two feet high. The *Carex tentaculata* is peculiar whitish-spiked.

JUNE 20, 1853
The bosky bank shows bright roses from its green recesses, the small white flowers of the panicled andromeda, beneath yellow lilies.

Found two lilies open in the very shallow inlet of the meadow. Exquisitely beautiful, and unlike anything else that we have is the first white lily just expanded in some shallow lagoon where the water is leaving it—perfectly fresh and pure before the insects have discovered it. How admirable its purity—how innocently sweet its fragrance. How significant that the rich black mud of our dead stream produces the water lily—out of that fertile slime springs this spotless purity. It is remarkable that those flowers which are most emblematical of purity should grow in the mud.

JUNE 21, 1852
The adder's tongue arethusa smells exactly like a snake. How singular

that in nature too beauty and offensiveness should be thus combined. In flowers as well as men we demand a beauty pure and fragrant, which perfumes the air. The flower which is showy but has no, or an offensive, odor expresses the character of too many mortals.

JUNE 21, 1853
Early on the morning of the 18th the river felt lukewarm to my fingers when my paddle dipped deeper than usual. The galium with three small white petals, *G. trifidum,* has been out some time. And I find that erectish broad-leaved three-nerved green-flowered one, perhaps *G. circaezans,* at Corner Spring.

JUNE 21, 1854
Mitchella in Deep Cut woods, probably a day or two. Its scent is agree-

maleberry (panicled andromeda, *Lyonia ligustrina*)

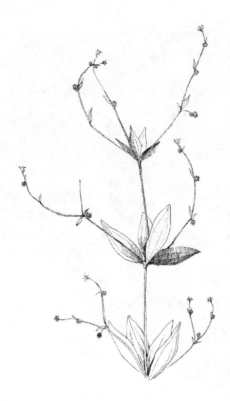

able and refreshing, between the mayflower and rum cherry bark, or like peach-stone meats. . . .

Indigo apparently a day in *some* places. Calopogon a day or two at least in Hubbard's Close—this handsomest of its family after the arethusa.

Again I am attracted by the deep scarlet of the wild moss rose half open in the grass—all glowing with rosy light.

JUNE 22, 1851

As I walk the railroad causeway, I notice that the fields and meadows have acquired various tinges as the season advances, the sun gradually using all his paints. There is the rosaceous evening red tinge of red clover like an evening sky gone down under the grass—the whiteweed tinge, the white clover tinge, which reminds me how sweet it smells. The tall buttercup stars the meadow on another side, telling of the wealth of dairies. The blue-eyed grass, so beautiful near at hand, imparts a kind of slate or clay blue tinge to the meads.

licorice bedstraw (*Galium circaezans*)

To Laurel Glen. . . . Yellow diervilla must have been in bloom about a week. Round-leaved cornel resembles the panicled in flower. The mountain laurel with its milk-white flower in cool and shady woods — reminds one of the vigor of nature. It is perhaps a first-rate flower — considering its size and ever-greenness. Its flower buds, curiously folded in a ten-angled pyramidal form are remarkable. . . . The Canada thistles begin to show their purple. What great thistle is that by the wall near Dakin's? Not yet in bloom. . . .

The beauty and fragrance of the wild rose are wholly agreeable and wholesome and wear well — and I do not wonder much that men have given the preference to this family of flowers notwithstanding their thorns. It is hardy and more complete in parts than most flowers — its color, buds, fragrance, leaves, the whole bush, frequently its stem in particular and finally its red or scarlet hips. . . . I take the wild rose buds to my chamber and put them in a pitcher of water and they will open there the next day, and a single flower will perfume a room — and then after a day the petals drop off and new buds open.

I am inclined to think that my hat, whose lining is gathered in midway so as to make a shelf, is about as good a botany box as I could have and far

grass pink
(*Calopogon pulchellus* = *C. tuberosus*)

mountain laurel (*Kalmia latifolia*)

bush-honeysuckle (yellow diervilla,
Diervilla trifida=D. lonicera)

more convenient, and there is something in the darkness and the vapors
that arise from the head—at least if you take a bath—which preserves
flowers through a long walk. Flowers will frequently come fresh out of this
botany box at the end of the day though they have had no sprinkling. . . .

Here is another pasture, with fields of sweet fern bushes—and the
humble but beautiful red lambkill everywhere alone or mingled with other
shrubs. Ever the walker will be attracted by some deeper red blossom
than usual. You cannot bring it home in good condition, else perchance it
would be better known. With white pines and birches, beginning to pre-
vail over the grass.

The *Specularia perfoliata* in flower at top of its leafy spikes for a few days on Clamshell Hill, this side oaks. It is a rich-colored and handsome-shaped sort of *lake* purple flower—or color of a lilac violet. The lower and earlier flowers have no corollas. Perhaps one of the first-rate flowers when many are open on the spike.

Motherwort by roadside probably yesterday. . . . In the warm noons nowadays, I see the spotted small yellow eyes of the four-leaved loosestrife looking at me from under the birches and pines springing up in sandy upland fields.

JUNE 23, 1854

Specularia handsome dark purple—on Cliffs—how long?

JUNE 24, 1852

I am disappointed to notice today that most of the pine tops incline to the west—as if the wind had to do with it. The panicled andromeda has froth on it. The *Linnaea borealis* just going out of blossom. I should have found it long ago. Its leaves densely cover the ground.

common motherwort (*Leonurus cardiaca*)

The *Specularia perfoliata,* clasping bellflower, on the Cliffs is very pretty and has apparently been out several days.

The lily is perhaps the only flower which all are eager to pluck, it may be partly because of its inaccessibility to most. The farmers' sons will frequently collect every bud that shows itself above the surface within half a mile. They are so infested by insects and it is so rare you get a perfect one which has opened itself—though these only are perfect—that the buds are commonly plucked and opened by hand. I have a faint recollection of pleasure derived from smoking dried lily stems before I was a man. I had commonly a supply of these. I have never smoked anything more noxious. I used to amuse myself with making the yellow drooping stamens rise and fall by blowing through the pores of the long stem. . . .

Under the cool glossy green leaves of small swamp white oaks, and leaning against their scaly bark near the water, you see the wild roses five

American twinflower (*Linnaea borealis*)

fireweed (*Epilobium angustifolium=Chamerion angustifolium*)

or six feet high looking forth from the shade—but almost every bush or copse near the river in low land which you approach these days emits the noisome odor of the carrion flower, so that you would think that all the dead dogs had drifted to that shore. All things both beautiful and ugly, agreeable and offensive, are expressed in flowers. All kinds and degrees of beauty, and all kinds of foulness. For what purpose has nature made a flower to fill the lowlands with the odor of carrion? Just so much beauty and virtue as there is in the world and just so much ugliness and vice you see expressed in flowers. Each human being has his flower, which expresses his character. In them nothing is concealed but everything published. Many a villager whose garden bounds on the river, when he approaches the willows and cornels by the river's edge, thinks that some carrion has lodged on his shore, when it is only the carrion flower he smells.

JUNE 27, 1852
The epilobium, spiked willow herb, shows its showy pale purple spires (pinkish?). It showed some color the 15th. I will set it down to the 20th. *Epilobium angustifolium,* one of the most conspicuous flowers at this season on dry open hillsides in the woods—sproutlands.

evening primrose (*Oenothera biennis*)

purple flowering raspberry (*Rubus odoratus*)

JUNE 28, 1852

Oenothera biennis, evening primrose—with its conspicuous flowers but rather unsightly stem and leaves. The *Rubus odoratus,* purple flowering raspberry, in gardens.

JUNE 29, 1851

There is a great deal of white clover this year. In many fields where there has been no clover seed sown for many years at least, it is more abundant than the red and the heads are nearly as large. Also pastures which are close cropped and where I think there was little or no clover last year are spotted white with a humbler growth. And everywhere by roadsides, garden borders, etc., even where the sward is trodden hard, the small white heads on short stems are sprinkled everywhere. As this is the season for the swarming of bees, and this clover is very attractive to them, it is probably the more difficult to secure them. At any rate it is the more important to secure their services now that they can make honey so fast. It is an interesting inquiry why this year is so favorable to the growth of clover! . . .

I look down on rays of prunella by the roadsides now. The panicled or privet andromeda with its fruit-like white flowers. Swamp pink I see for the first time this season. . . .

The panicled cornel [gray dogwood, *Cornus racemosa*], a low shrub, in blossom by wall sides now.

JUNE 29, 1852

Leonurus Cardiaca, motherwort, a nettle-like plant by the streetside. . . . It is pleasant to remember those quiet Sabbath mornings by remote stagnant rivers and ponds—when pure white water lilies just expanded, not yet infested by insects, float on the waveless water and perfume the atmosphere. Nature never appears more serene and innocent and fragrant. A hundred white lilies open to the sun rest on the surface smooth as oil amid their pads, while devil's-needles are glancing over them. It requires some skill so to pull a lily as to get a long stem. The great yellow lily, the spatterdock, expresses well the fertility of the river.

The *Sparganium ramosum* [*S. eurycarpum*] or bur-reed amid the flags now. It is associated with the reed mace by systematists. One flower on a spike of the *Pontederia cordata* just ready to expand. . . . The *Anemone Virginiana,* tall anemone, looking like a white buttercup, on Egg Rock, cannot have been long in bloom. I see the columbine lingering still.

JUNE 30, 1851

The blue flag (*Iris versicolor*) enlivens the meadow. . . .

The cranberry is now in blossom. Their fresh shoots have run a foot or two over the surface.

JUNE 30, 1852

Is not this period more than any distinguished for flowers? When roses, swamp pinks, morning glories, arethusas, pogonias, orchises, blue flags, epilobiums, mountain laurel, and white lilies are all in blossom at once!

JULY 1, 1852

Roses are in their prime now, growing amid huckleberry bushes, ferns, and sweet ferns, especially about some dry pond hole—some paler some more red. Methinks they must have bloomed in vain while only wild men roamed. Yet now they only adorn these cows' pasture. . . . We pushed our

pickerelweed (*Pontederia cordata*)

boat into the midst of some shallow bays, where the water, not more than a foot deep, was covered with pads and spotted white with many hundreds of lilies which had just expanded. Yet perhaps there was not one open which had not an insect in it, and most had some hundreds of small gnats, which, however, we shook out without much trouble, instead of drowning them out, which makes the petals close.

The freshly opened lilies were a pearly white, and though the water amid the pads was quite unrippled, the passing air gave a slight oscillating, boat-like motion to and fro to the flowers, like boats held fast by their cables. Some of the lilies had a beautiful rosaceous tinge, most conspicuous in the half-opened flower, extending through the calyx to the second row of petals, on those parts of the petals between the calyx leaves which were most exposed to the influence of the light. They were tinged with red, as they are very commonly tinged with green, as if there were a gradual transition from the stamens to the petals. It seemed to be referred to the same coloring principle which is seen in the undersides of the pads as well

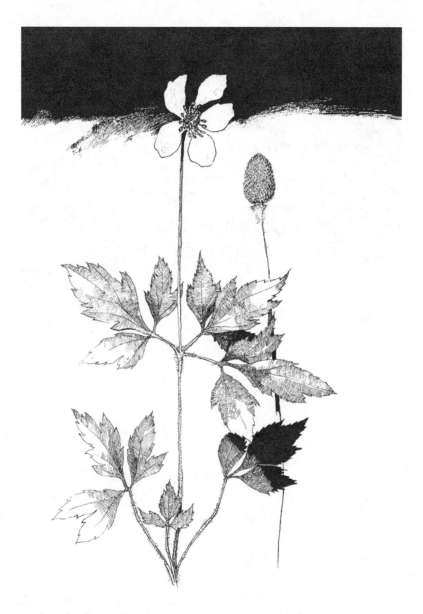

as the calyx leaves. Yet these rosaceous ones are chiefly interesting to me
for variety, and I am contented that lilies should be white and leave those
higher colors to the land. I wished to breathe the atmosphere of lilies, and
get the full impression which lilies are fitted to make. . . .

   After eating our luncheon at Rice's landing, we observed that every
white lily in the river was shut—and they remained so all the afternoon,

tall anemone (*Anemone virginiana*)

blue flag (*Iris versicolor*)

though it was no more sunny nor cloudy than the forenoon, except some which I had plucked before noon and cast into the river, which floating down lodged amid the pondweed, which continued fresh but had not the power to close their petals. It would be interesting to observe how instantaneously these lilies close at noon. I only observed that, though there were myriads fully open before I ate my lunch at noon, after dinner I could not find one open anywhere for the rest of the day. . . . Found the *Polygonum sagittatum,* scratchgrass, just blossoming in the meadows, and an abundance of the marsh speedwell and of pogonia (adder's tongue arethusas).

Last night as I lay awake I dreamed of the muddy and weedy river on which I had been paddling—and I seemed to derive some vigor from my day's experience like the lilies which have their roots at the bottom.

I have plucked a white lily bud just ready to expand and after keeping it in water for two days (till July 3d) have turned back its petals with my hand and touched the lapped points of the petals when they sprang open—and rapidly expanded in my hand into a perfect blossom with the petals as perfectly disposed at equal intervals as on their native lakes, and in this case of course untouched by an insect. I cut its stem short and placed it in a broad dish of water, where it sailed about under the breath of the beholder with a slight undulatory motion. The breeze of his half-suppressed admiration it was that filled its sail. It was a rose-tinted one. A kind of popular aura that may be trusted methinks. Men will travel to the Nile to see the lotus flower, who have never seen in their glory the lotuses of their native streams. . . .

arrow-vine (*Polygonum sagittatum*=*Persicaria sagittata*)

At the bathing place there is [a] hummock which was floated on to the meadow some springs ago—now densely covered with the handsome red-stemmed wild rose, a full but irregular clump, from the ground, show-ing no bare stems below, but a dense mass of shining leaves and small red stems above in their midst, and on every side now in the twilight more than usually beautiful they appear. Countless roses partly closed of a very deep rich color, as if the rays of the departed sun still shone through them—a more spiritual rose at this hour, beautifully blushing, and then the unspeakable beauty and promise of those fair swollen buds that spot the mass which will blossom tomorrow, and the more distant promise of the handsomely formed green ones, which yet show no red, for few things are handsomer than a rosebud in any stage. These mingled with a few pure white elder blossoms and some rosaceous or pinkish meadow-sweet heads.

black elderberry (*Sambucus nigra*)

JULY 2, 1854

An abundance of red lilies in the upland dry meadow, near Smith's Spring trough. Low from one to two feet high, upright-flowered, more or less dark shade of red-freckled and sometimes wrinkle-edged petals—must have been some days. This has come with the intense summer heats, a torrid July heat like a red sunset threatening torrid heat. (Do we not always have a dry time just before the huckleberries turn?)

JULY 2, 1857

Calla palustris (with its convolute point like the cultivated) at the south end of Gowing's Swamp. Having found this in one place I now find it in another. Many an object is not seen though it falls within the range of our visual ray, because it does not come within the range of our intellectual ray—i.e. we are not looking for it. So in the largest sense, we find only the world we look for.

JULY 3, 1852

The yellow lily *Lilium Canadense* [Canada lily] is out, rising above the meadow grass sometimes one sometimes two. Young woodchucks sitting in their holes allow me to come quite near. Clover is mostly dried up. The *Chimaphila umbellata,* wintergreen, must have been in blossom some time. The back side of its petals "cream colored tinged with purple," which is turned toward the beholder while the face is toward the earth, is the handsomest. It is a very pretty little chandelier of a flower fit to adorn the forest floor. . . . The common carrot by the roadside, *Daucus carota,* is in some respects an interesting plant—for its umbel as Bigelow says is shaped like a bird's nest, and its large pinnatifid involucre interlacing by its fine segments resembles a fanciful ladies' workbasket.

JULY 3, 1854

The river and shores with their pads and weeds are now in their midsummer and hot weather condition, now when the pontederias have just begun to bloom. The seething river is confined within two burnished borders of pads, gleaming in the sun for a mile, and a sharp snap is heard from them from time to time. Next stands the upright phalanx of dark green pontederias.

When I have left the boat a short time the seats become intolerably hot. . . . A coneflower (new plant) *Rudbeckia hirta* (except that I call its disk not

Queen Anne's lace (*Daucus carota*)

dull brown but dull or dark purple or maroon in Arethusa Meadow. (However, Wood calls it dark purple.) Saw one plucked June 25—blossomed probably about that time. Many yesterday in meadows beyond almshouse. Probably introduced lately from West.

JULY 3, 1859
The *Mitchella repens*, so abundant now in the northwest part of Hubbard's Grove, emits a strong astringent cherry-like scent as I walk over it now that it is so abundantly in bloom, which is agreeable to me—spotting the ground with its downy-looking white flowers.

JULY 4, 1852
The great spatterdock lily is a rich yellow at a little distance and seen lying on its great pads it is an indispensable evidence of the fertility of the river.

JULY 4, 1860
The large johnswort now begins to be noticed generally—a July yellow.

The vetch-like flower by the Marlborough road, the *Tephrosia Virginica* [goat's-rue, *T. virginiana*] is in blossom with mixed red and yellowish blossoms.

Also the white fine-flowered Jersey tea, *Ceanothus Americana*. And by the side of woodpaths the humble cow-wheat, *Apocynum,* etc. . . .

black-eyed Susan (*Rudbeckia hirta*)

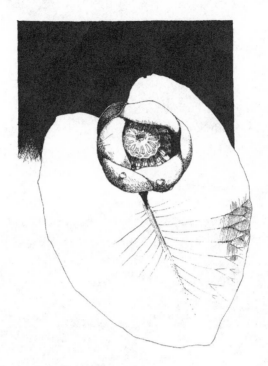

bullhead lily (spatterdock, *Nuphar variegata*)

The flowers of the umbelled pyrola or common wintergreen are really very handsome now, dangling red from their little umbels like jewelry—especially the unexpanded buds with their red calyx leaves against the white globe of petals. . . .

The calamint grows by the land beyond Seven-Star Lane—now in blossom.

JULY 5, 1852
How fitting to have every day in a vase of water on your table the wild-flowers of the season which are just blossoming. Can any house [be] said to be furnished without them?

JULY 5, 1854
The bluecurls and fragrant everlasting with their refreshing aroma show themselves now pushing up in dry fields—bracing to the thought. Horse-mint under Clamshell, apparently yesterday. On Lupine Knoll picked up a dark-colored spearhead three and a half inches long lying on the bare sand—so hot that I could not long hold it tight in my hand.

The large evening primrose—below the foot of our garden—does not open till some time between 6:30 and 8:00 P.M. or sundown. It was not open when I went to bathe, but partly out in the cool of the evening at sundown, as if enjoying the serenity of the hour.

The red clover heads are now turned black. They no longer impart that rosaceous tinge to the meadows and fertile fields. It is but a short time that their rich bloom lasts.

The white is black or withering also. Whiteweed still looks white in the fields. Blue-eyed grass is now rarely seen. The grass in the fields and meadows is not so fresh and fair as it was a fortnight ago. It is drier and riper and ready for the mowers. Now June is past. June is the month for grass and flowers. Now grass is turning to hay, and flowers to fruits.

Lysimachia stricta, upright loosestrife, now well out by Hosmer's Pond and

New Jersey tea (Jersey tea,
Ceanothus americanus)

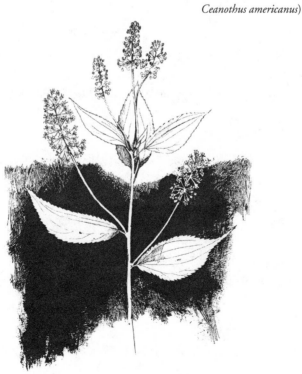

mountain mint (calamint, *Pycnanthemum muticum*)

elsewhere, a rather handsome flower — or cylindrical raceme of flowers. . . .
The red lily, *Lilium Philadelphicum*. This has very open petals of a dark
vermilion color, freckled within, and grows in rather dry places, by woodpaths, etc., and is very interesting and handsome.

JULY 6, 1854
Now a great show of elder blossoms.

JULY 6, 1856
There is a young red mulberry in the lower hedge beneath the celtis.

The heartleaf flower is now very conspicuous and pretty (3 P.M.) in that pool westerly of the old Conantum house. Its little white five-petaled flower, about the size of a five-cent piece, looks like a little white lily. Its perfectly heart-shaped floating leaf an inch or more long is the smallest kind of pad. There is a single pad to each slender stem (which is from one to several feet long in proportion to the depth of the water) and these pad-lets cover sometimes like an imbrication the whole surface of a pool. Close under each leaf or pad is concealed an umbel of ten to fifteen flower buds of various ages, and of these one at a time (and sometimes more) curls upward between the lobes of the base, and expands its corolla to the light and air about half an inch above the water—and so on successively till all

swamp candles (upright loosestrife, *Lysimachia stricta=L. terrestris*)

wood lily (*Lilium philadelphicum*)

have flowered. Over the whole surface of the shallow pool you see thus each little pad with its pretty lily between its lobes, turned toward the sun. It is simply leaf and flower.

JULY 7, 1852
Lepidium Virginicum, peppergrass, an inconspicuous weed, with seed vessels somewhat like shepherd's purse. . . .

When the yellow lily flowers in the meadows and the red in dry lands and by woodpaths, then methinks the flowering season has reached its height. They surprise me as perhaps no more can. Now I seem prepared for anything.

JULY 8, 1851
The thick heads of the yellow dock warn me of the lapse of time.

red mulberry (*Morus rubra*)

wild peppergrass (*Lepidium virginicum*)

JULY 9, 1852

Those white water lilies, what boats! I toss one into the pan half unfolded and it floats upright like a boat. It is beautiful when half open and also when fully expanded. . . . The red lily with its torrid color and sun-freckled spots, dispensing too with the outer garment of a calyx, its petals so open and wide apart that you can see through it in every direction, tells of hot weather. It is a handsome bell shape, so upright, and the *flower* prevails over every other part. It belongs not to spring. It grows in the path by the town bound. . . . At Clematis Pond, the small arrowhead in the mud is still bleeding where cows have cropped. In some places the mud is covered with the *Ilysanthes gratioloides,* false pimpernel. I think it is this, the *flower* shaped somewhat like a skullcap (*Lindernia* of Bigelow).

JULY 10, 1852

It is with a suffocating sensation and a slight pain in the head that I walk

false pimpernel
(*Ilysanthes gratioloides=Lindernia dubia*)

white sweet clover (*Melilotus leucantha=M. albus*)

the Union Turnpike where the heat is reflected from the road . . . I find the white melilot, *Melilotus leucantha,* a fragrant clover in blossom by this roadside.

St. John's wort is perhaps the prevailing flower now. Many fields are very yellow with it.

JULY 10, 1857

The tephrosia which grows by Peter's road in the woods is a very striking and interesting, if I may not say beautiful, flower — especially when as here it is seen in a cool and shady place, its clear rose purple contrasting very agreeably with yellowish white, rising from amidst a bed of finely pinnate leaves.

JULY 11, 1852

Morning glories are in perfection now, some dense masses of this vine with very red flowers, very attractive and cool looking in dry mornings. They are very tender and soon defaced in a nosegay. The large orange lily with sword-shaped leaves strayed from cultivation by the roadside beyond the stone bridge.

The bass on Conantum is now well in blossom. It probably commenced about the 9th. Its flowers are conspicuous for a tree and a rather agreeable odor fills the air. The tree resounds with the hum of bees on the flowers. . . .

Pogonias and calopogons are very abundant in the meadows. They are interesting if only for their high color. Any redness is after all rare and precious. It is the color of our blood. The rose owes its preeminence in great measure to its color. It is said to be from the Celtic *rhos,* red. It is nature's most precious color.

JULY 11, 1857
The cymbidium [grass pink] is really a splendid flower—with its spike, two or three inches long of *commonly* three or five large *irregular* concave

orange day-lily (*Hemerocallis fulva*)

linden (American basswood, *Tilia americana*)

star-shaped purple flowers, amid the cool green meadow grass. It has an agreeable fragrance withal.

I see more berries than usual of the *Rubus triflorus* in the open meadow near the southeast corner of the Hubbard meadow blueberry swamp. Call it perhaps Cymbidium Meadow. They are dark shining red—and when ripe of a very agreeable flavor and somewhat of the raspberry's *spirit*.

JULY 12, 1856

In Moore's meadow by Turnpike see the vetch in purple patches weighing down the grass, as if a purple tinge were reflected there. White vervain. Smooth sumac apparently yesterday. Rue is beginning now to whiten the meadows on all hands. . . .

Red lilies in prime—single upright fiery flowers, their throats how splendidly and *variously* spotted, hardly two of quite the same hue and not two spotted alike. Leopard spotted. Averaging a foot or more in height. Amid the huckleberry and lambkill, etc., in the moist, meadowy pasture.

JULY 13, 1852

Already the goldenrod, apparently *Solidago stricta,* willow-leaved golden-rod, preaches of the lapse of time on the Walden road. How many a tale its yellow tells! . . . Succory or *Cichorium intybus*.[7] It appears to shut up this hot weather.

2 P.M. — To Little Truro.
You now especially notice some very red fields when the redtop grass grows luxuriantly and is now in full flower — a red purple passing into brown, looking at a distance like a red-sandstone soil. The different cultivated fields are thus like so many different colored checkers on a checkerboard.

First we had the June grass reddish brown and the sorrel red of June — now the *redtop red* of July.

Saw something blue, or glaucous, in Beck Stow's Swamp today, approached and discovered the *Andromeda Polifolia*. In the midst of the swamp at the north end. Not long since out of bloom. This is another

chicory (succory, *Cichorium intybus*)

instance of a common experience. When I am shown from abroad—or hear of, or in any [way] become interested in, some plant or other thing I am pretty sure to find it soon. Within a week R.W.E. showed me a slip of this in a botany, as a great rarity which George Bradford brought from Watertown. I had long been interested in it by Linnaeus' account. I now find it in abundance. It is a neat and tender-looking plant, with the pearly new shoots now half a dozen inches long and the singular narrow revolute leaves. I suspect the flower does not add much to it.

JULY 15, 1854

We seem to be passing or to have passed a dividing line between spring and autumn, and begin to descend the long slope toward winter. On the shady side of the hill I go along Hubbard's walls toward the bathing place—stepping high to keep my feet as dry as may be. (All is stillness in the fields.) The calamint, *Pycnanthemum muticum,* standing by the wall with its hoary upper leaves—full of light even this cloudy day, and reminding of the fragrance which I know so well—is an agreeable sight. I need not smell it. It is balm to my mind to remember its fragrance. . . . There are many butterflies, yellow and red, about the *Asclepias incarnata* now.

JULY 16, 1850

I have not yet been able to collect half a thimble full of the pollen of the pine on Walden, abundant as it was last summer.

There is in our yard a little pitch pine four or five years old and not much more than a foot high, with small cones on it but no male flowers yet, and I do not know of another pitch pine tree within half a mile.

JULY 16, 1851

The meadowsweet is now in bloom and the yarrow prevails by all roadsides. I see the hardhack too, homely but dear plant—just opening its red clustered flowers. The small aster too now abounds, *Aster miser*—and the tall buttercup still. . . . The prunella sends back a blue ray from under my feet as I walk—the pale lobelia too. . . . The heart-leaved loosestrife, *Lysimachia ciliata,* is seen in low open woods. . . . The dog's-bane has a pretty delicate bell-like flower. . . . Nightshade is in blossom. Came through the pine plains behind James Baker's where late was open pasture, now open pitch pine woods—only here and there the grass has given place to a carpet of pine needles. These are among our pleasantest woods—open, level, with blackberry vines interspersed and flowers, as lady's slippers earlier, and pinks.

Xyris, yellow-eyed grass, with three pretty yellow petals atop. The forget-me-not is still abundant. . . .

The bass on Conantum is a very rich sight now. . . . Its twigs are drooping, weighed down with pendulous flowers, so that, when you stand directly under it and look up you see one mass of flowers, a flowery canopy. Its conspicuous leaf-like bracts too have the effect of flowers. The tree resounds with the hum of bees—bumblebees and honeybees. Rose bugs and

swamp milkweed (*Asclepias incarnata*)

fringed loosestrife (*Lysimachia ciliata*)

butterflies also are here, a perfect susurrus, a sound as C. says unlike any other in nature — not like the wind as that is like the sea. The bees abound on the flowers of the smooth sumac now. The branches of this tree touch the ground, and it has somewhat the appearance of being weighed down with flowers. The air is full of sweetness. The tree is full of poetry.

JULY 16, 1854
The large (?) circaea (it is the *lutetiana,* though the flowers are white) apparently two or three days.

JULY 17, 1856
Under the oak in Brown's moraine pasture by Water Dock Meadow, a great arum more than three feet high — like a tropical plant in open land with leaflets more than a foot long. There is richweed there, apparently not quite out.

Am caught in the rain and take shelter under the thick white pine by Lee's Cliff. I see there—under—an abundance of chimaphila in bloom. It is a beautiful flower, with its naked umbel of crystalline purplish white flowers, their disks at an angle with the horizon. On its lower side a ring of purple (or crimson) scales at the base of its concave petals around the large green sticky ovary.

JULY 18, 1852
We are gliding swiftly up the river by Lee's Bend. The surface of the water is the place to see the pontederia from, for now the spikes of flowers are all brought into a dense line—a heavy line of blue a foot or more in width—on one or both sides of the river. The pontederias are now in their prime. There being no withered heads, they are very freshly blue. In the sun when you are looking west they are of a violaceous blue.

common yellow-eyed grass
(*Xyris difformis*)

forget-me-not (*Myosotis* spp.)

JULY 18, 1854

Methinks the asters and goldenrods begin, like the early ripening leaves, with midsummer heats. Now look out for these children of the sun. When already the fall of some of the very earliest spring flowers has commenced. . . . By the elecampane and the Wheeler house to my great surprise growing abundantly in the road the *Monarda fistulosa*—apparently a week at least.

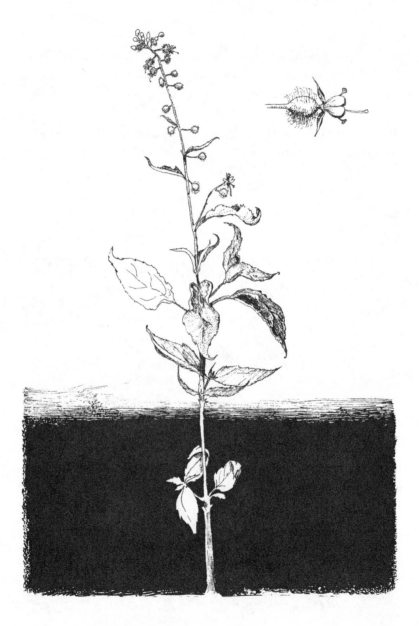

Three or more feet high with a few heads containing a whorl of large very showy crimson flowers with crimsoned bracts in whorls beneath—with a balm or summer savory or sweet marjoram fragrance. These things out of the heavenward northwest. . . .

We have very few bass trees in Concord—but walk near them at this season and they will be betrayed though several rods off by the wonderful susurrus of the bees, etc. which their flowers attract. It is worth going a long way to hear. I was warned that I was passing one in two instances on the river—the only two I passed—by this remarkable sound. At a little distance it is like the sound of a waterfall or of the cars—close at hand like a factory full of looms. They were chiefly humblebees, and the great globose tree was all alive with them. I heard the murmur distinctly fifteen rods off. You will know if you pass within a few rods of a bass tree at this season in any part of the town by this loud murmur like a waterfall which proceeds from it.

JULY 18, 1860

The *Asclepias Cornuti* is abundantly visited nowadays by a large orange brown butterfly with dark spots and with *silver* spots beneath. Wherever an asclepias grows you see them.

JULY 19, 1851

Methinks my seasons revolve more slowly than those of nature. I am differently timed. I am—contented. This rapid revolution of nature, even of nature in me, why should it hurry me? Let a man step to the music which he hears, however measured. Is it important that I should mature as soon as an apple tree? Yea, as soon as an oak? . . .

Already the goldenrod is budded, but I can make no haste for that. . . . Today I met with the first orange flower of autumn. What means this doubly torrid, this Bengal tint? Yellow took sun enough—but this is the fruit of a dog-day sun. The year has but just produced it. Here is the Canada thistle in bloom visited by butterflies and bees. The butterflies have swarmed within these few days especially about the milkweeds. The swamp pink still fills the air with its perfume in swamps and by the causeways—though it is far gone. The wild rose still scatters its petals over the

large enchanter's nightshade (*Circaea lutetiana=C. canadensis*)

leaves of neighboring plants. The wild morning glory or bindweed with its delicate red and white blossoms. I remember it ever as a goblet full of purest morning air and sparkling with dew, showing the dewpoint, winding round itself for want of other support. It grows by the Hubbard Bridge causeway near the angelica.

wild bergamot (*Monarda fistulosa*)

JULY 19, 1854

Apparently a catbird's nest in a shrub oak, lined with root fibers, with three green-blue eggs. *Erigeron annuus* perhaps fifteen rods or more beyond the Hawthorn Bridge on right hand—a new plant, probably last month. Thinner leaves than the *strigosus*.

JULY 19, 1860

You see now great beds of polygonums above the surface getting ready to bloom, and the dulichium [three-way sedge, *D. arundinaceum*] stands

common milkweed (*Asclepias cornuti=A. syriaca*)

wild morning glory (*Calystegia sepium*)

thick in shallow water. While in the cultivated ground the pigweed, butter-weed, and Roman wormwood and amaranth are now rank and conspicu-ous weeds. . . .

The rich crimson undersides (with their regularly branching veins) of some white lily pads surpasses the color of most flowers. No wonder the spiders are red that swim beneath. I think of the fishes that swim beneath this crimson canopy—beneath a crimson sky. I can frequently trace the passage of a boat, a pickerel fisher perhaps, by the crimson undersides of the pads upturned.

The pads crowd and overlap each other in most amicable fashion. Sometimes one lobe of a yellow lily pad is above its neighbor while the other is beneath, and frequently I see where a little heartleaf (now showing its green spidery rays) has emerged by the stem in the sinus of a great nuphar leaf and is outspread in the very midst of it. The pads are rapidly consumed—but fresh ones are all the while pushing up and unrolling. They push up and spread out in the least crevice that offers.

JULY 20, 1852

Perceived a small weed coming up all over the fields which has an aromatic scent. Did not at first discover that it was bluecurls. It is a little affecting

daisy fleabane (*Erigeron annuus*)

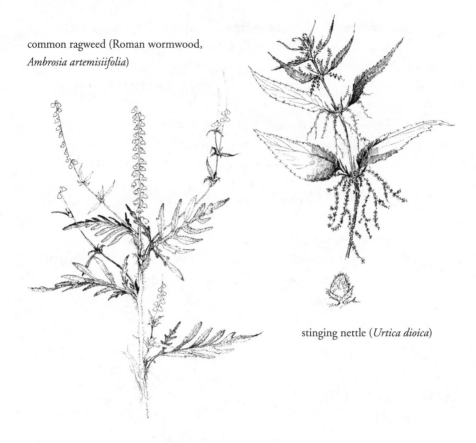

common ragweed (Roman wormwood, *Ambrosia artemisiifolia*)

stinging nettle (*Urtica dioica*)

that the year should be thus solemn and regular, that this weed should have withheld itself so long, biding its appointed time, and now without fail be coming up all over the land, still extracting that well-known aroma out of the elements, to adorn its part of the year! I also perceive one of the coarse late fleabanes making itself conspicuous. The stinging nettle is not very obvious, methinks. . . .

Is that nettle-like but smooth and I should say obtusely four-angled plant in the low moist ground on the Assabet the *Boehmeria cylindrica? Alisma Plantago,* water plantain, about out of flower, by the Assabet—small leaves like the plantain.

JULY 21, 1851
The dusty mayweed now blooms by the roadside, one of the humblest flowers.

The rough hawkweed too by the damp roadside, resembling in its flower the autumnal dandelion. That was probably the *Verbena hastata* or common blue vervain which I found the other day by Walden Pond.

JULY 21, 1852

At sunset to Corner Spring.

A broken strain from a bobolink. A golden robin once or twice today. The *Mimulus ringens,* or monkeyflower—one of the most noticeable of this class of flowers.

JULY 21, 1853

Went in pursuit of boys who had stolen my boat seat, to Fair Haven. . . . There is no more beautiful part of the river than the entrance to this pond. The *Asclepias incarnata* is well named water silkweed, for it grows here amid the buttonbushes and willows in the wettest places along the river.

false nettle (*Boehmeria cylindrica*)

water plantain (*Alisma triviale*)

Nature is beautiful only as a place where a life is to be lived. It is not beautiful to him who has not resolved on a beautiful life. The horned utricularia appears to be in its prime, though there was none here June 16th. It yellows the shore together with the hyssop and filiform ranunculus, not to mention the lanceolate loosestrife. The spear thistle.

The tall anemone grows by the red oak near the elms opposite the pond on Conantum and is still in flower. I am surprised by the abundance of large shining blackberries on the hillsides—every bush does its best.

JULY 21, 1859

The pontederia on the Assabet is a very fresh and clear blue today and in its *early* prime—very handsome to see. The nesaea grows commonly along the river near the powder mills—one very dense bed of it at the mouth of the powder mill canal.

JULY 22, 1852

Tansy is now conspicuous by the roadsides, covered with small red butterflies. It is not an uninteresting plant. I probably put it a little too early.

Is that a slender bellflower with entire leaves by the Corner road? The green berries of the arum are seen, and the now *reddish* fruit of the trillium, and the round pea-sized green berries of the axil-flowering Solomon's seal. Farmers have commenced their meadow haying. . . . The *Rhus glabra* flowers are covered with bees, *large* yellowish wasps, and butterflies—they are all alive with them. How much account insects make of some flowers! There are other botanists than I. . . . *Galium circaezans,* wild liquorice, in Baker Farm Swamp.

JULY 22, 1860

The next field on the west slopes gently from both east and west to a meadow in the middle. So as I look over the wall it is first *dark green* where white clover has been cut (still showing a myriad low white heads which resound with the hum of bees). Next along the edge of the bottom or meadow is a strip or belt three or four rods wide of redtop—uncut, perfectly distinct. Then the cheerful bright yellow sedge of the meadow, yellow almost as gamboge. Then a corresponding belt of redtop on its upper

bull thistle (spear thistle, *Cirsium lanceolatum*=*C. vulgare*)

edge—quite straight and rectilinear like the first. Then a glaucous green field of grain still quite low. And in the further corner of the field a much darker square of green than any yet, all brilliant in this wonderful light. You thus have a sort of terrestrial rainbow, thus:

The farmer accustomed to look at his crops from a mercenary point of view is not aware how beautiful they are. This prospect was really exciting even as a rainbow is.

JULY 23, 1853

About the water further north the elodea [marsh St. John's-wort, *Triadenum virginicum*] is very common, and there too the rhexia is seen afar on the islets—its brilliant red like a rose. It is fitly called meadow beauty. Is it not the handsomest and most striking and brilliant flower since roses and lilies began? Blue vervain out some days.

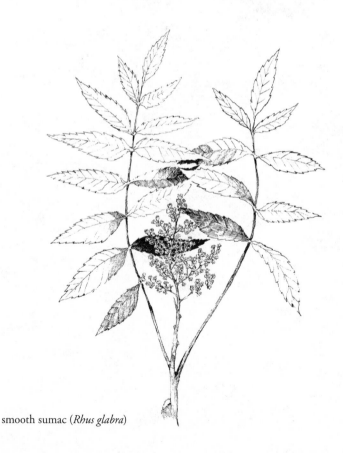

smooth sumac (*Rhus glabra*)

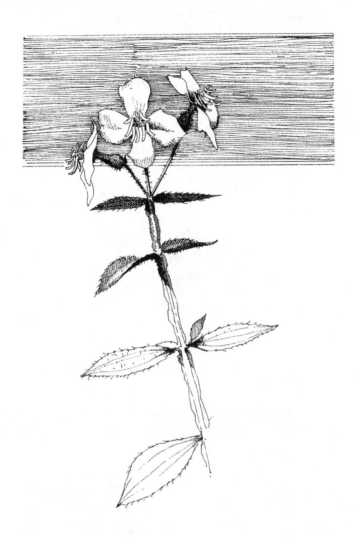

JULY 23, 1860

The late rose is now in prime along the river—a pale rose color but very delicate, keeping up the memory of roses.

JULY 24, 1853

How far behind the spring seems now—farther off perhaps than ever—for this heat and dryness is most opposed to spring. Where most I sought for flowers in April and May I do not think to go now—it is either drought and barrenness or fall there now. The reign of moisture is long since over.

meadow beauty (*Rhexia virginica*)

For a long time the year feels the influence of the snows of winter and the long rains of spring, but now how changed! It is like another and a fabulous age to look back on. When earth's veins were full of moisture and violets burst out on every hillside.

JULY 25, 1853
Dodder, probably the 21st. Bluecurls. Burdock, probably yesterday. . . .

Those New Hampshire–like pastures near Asa Melvin's are covered or dotted with bunches of indigo still in bloom more numerously than anywhere that I remember.

JULY 25, 1854
The long chestnut flowers have fallen and strew the road. *Arabis Canadensis,* sicklepod, still in flower and with pods not quite two inches long. Pennyroyal, a day or two.

JULY 25, 1856
Whorled utricularia very abundantly out, apparently in its prime.

blue vervain (*Verbena hastata*)

I reckon that about nine tenths of the flowers of the year have now blossomed. . . . The smaller purple-fringed orchis has not quite filled out its spike. What a surprise to detect under the dark damp cavernous copse, where some wild beast might fitly prowl, this splendid flower silently standing with all its eyes on you. It has a rich fragrance withal.

American chestnut (*Castanea vesca=C. dentata*)

JULY 26, 1856

Smaller bur-reed (*Sparganium Americanum*), apparently a few days.

JULY 27, 1852

It is very pleasant to walk up and down the stream however studying the further bank—which is six or seven feet high and completely covered with verdure of various kinds. . . . *Viburnum dentatum* [smooth arrowwood], elder, and red-stemmed cornel [red osier, *Cornus stolonifera*], all with an abundance of green berries help clothe the bank—and the *Asclepias incarnata* and meadow rue fill the crevices. *Above all* there is the cardinal flower just opened, close to the water's edge—remarkable for its intense scarlet color, contrasting with the surrounding green.

floating bladderwort (*Utriculata inflata=U. radiata*)

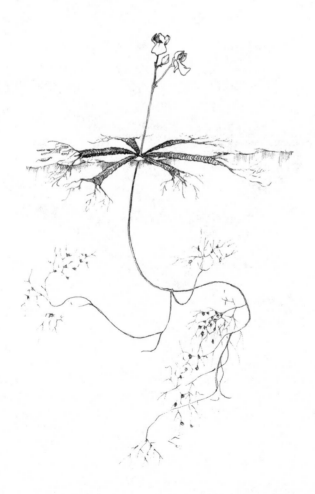

common bur-reed (*Sparganium americanum*)

JULY 28, 1852

There is a yellowish light now from a low tufted yellowish broad-leaved grass in fields that have been mown. A June-like breezy air. The large shaped sagittaria out, a large crystalline-white three-petaled flower.

JULY 28, 1858

From wall corner saw a pinkish patch on sidehill west of Baker Farm, which turned out to be epilobium a rod across. Through the glass it was as fine as a moss but with the naked eye it might have been mistaken for a

dead pine bough. This pink flower was distinguished perhaps three quarters of a mile.

JULY 29, 1852

I see a bluet still in damp ground. Apples now by their size remind me of the harvest. I see a few roses in moist places with short curved thorns and narrow bracts. *Eupatorium perfoliatum* just beginning. . . .

Bluecurls and wormwood springing up everywhere with their aroma—especially the first—are quite restorative. It is time we had a little wormwood to flavor the somewhat tasteless or cloying summer, which palls upon the taste.

boneset (*Eupatorium perfoliatum*)

At Vernonia Meadow I notice the beds of horsemint now in flower—bluish whorls of flowers now in its prime. Now is the time to gather thoroughwort. Cardinals are in their prime. The hibiscus is barely budded but already the meadow hay mowers have sheared close to it. . . . The sight of the small rough sunflower about a dry ditch bank and hedge advances me at once further toward autumn. At the same time I hear a dry ripe autumnal chirp of a cricket. It is the next step to the first goldenrod. It grows where it escapes the mower—but no doubt in our localities of plants we do not know where they would prefer to grow if unmolested by man, but rather where they best escape his vandalism. . . .

Crossed over to Tuttle's. Aaron's rod not yet. The high blackberries *began* to be ripe about a week ago. The *small* flowers of the *Helianthemum Canadense* (cistus). Its leaves are like the *Lechea major* [hairy pinweed, *L. mucronata*], for which I took it last (?) fall, when surrounded with frost at its base, hence called frostweed.

wild mint (horsemint, *Mentha canadensis*)

The *Cyperus dentatus* [bulblet sedge] in bloom on hard sandy parts of meadows is very interesting and handsome on being inspected now, with its bright chestnut purple *sided* flat spikelets. A plant and color looking toward autumn. Very neat and handsome on a close inspection.

JULY 30, 1852

Do not all flowers that blossom after mid-July remind us of the fall? After midsummer we have a belated feeling as if we had all been idlers—and are forward to see in each sight, and hear in each sound some presage of the fall. Just as in middle age man anticipates the end of life. Tansy is a prevalent flower now—dog's-bane still common. . . .

frostweed (rock-rose, *Helianthemum canadense*=*Crocanthemum canadense*)

The *Clethra alnifolia* is just beginning (as the swamp pink shows its last white petals) but August will have its beauty. It is important as one of the later flowers. High blackberries ripe, apparently for a day or two. That succulent plant by Tuttle's sluice appears to be *Sedum Telephium,* garden orpine or live-forever, called also houseleek, since it will grow if only one end is tucked under a shingle.

JULY 30, 1853
Lygodium palmatum [climbing fern] now apparently in bloom. It is a most beautiful slender and delicate fern twining like vine about the stem of the meadowsweet, panicled andromeda, goldenrods, etc. to the height of three feet or more and difficult to detach from them. The lower half in the

common highbush blackberry
(*Rubus allegheniensis*)

purple orpine (live-forever,
Sedum telephium=Hylotelephium telephium)

slender-leaved gerardia (*Gerardia tenuifolia=Agalinis tenuifolia*)

shade of small leafy sterile frondlets, the upper half exposed to the light of the finely divided fertile frondlets. Our most beautiful fern—and most suitable for wreaths or garlands. It is rare.[8]

JULY 31, 1853
Purple gerardia by tomorrow or the next day—the linear-leafed gerardia. . . . I calculate that less than forty species of flowers known to me remain to blossom this year.

JULY 31, 1856
As I am going across to Bear Garden Hill, I see much *white Polygala sanguinea* [purple milkwort] with the red in A. Wheeler's meadow (next to Potter's). Also much of the *Bartonia tenella* which has been out *some days* at least, five rods from ditch and three from Potter's fence.

The berries of what I have called the alternate-leaved cornel are now ripe—
a very dark blue, blue-black and round, but dropping off prematurely
leaving handsome *red* cymes, which adorn the trees from a distance.
Chelone glabra just out.

Groundnut well out.[9]

Virginia screwstem (*Bartonia tenella=B. virginica*)

pagoda dogwood (*Cornus alternifolia*)

groundnut (*Apios americana*)

AUGUST 1, 1855

Pennyroyal and alpine enchanter's nightshade well out, how long?

AUGUST 1, 1856

The Great Meadows being a little wet—hardly as much as usual, I took off my shoes and went barefoot some two miles through the cut-grass. . . . The cut-grass is bad for tender feet, and you must be careful not to let it draw through your hands, for it will cut like a fine saw. I was surprised to see dense beds of rhexia in full bloom there, apparently on hummocks one rod in diameter left by the ice, or in long ridges mixed with ferns and some *Lysimachia lanceolata,* arrowhead, etc. They make a splendid show, these brilliant rose-colored patches. . . . It is about the richest color to be seen now. Yet few ever see them in this perfection—unless the haymaker who levels them or the birds that fly over the meadow. These gay standards otherwise unfurled in vain.

AUGUST 1, 1860

The immediate and raised edge of the river with its willows and button-bushes and polygonums is a light green, but the immediately adjacent low meadows where the sedge prevails is a brilliant and cheerful yellow, intensely, incredibly bright—such color as you never see in pictures. Yellow of various tints, in the lowest and sedgiest parts deepening to so much color as if gamboges had been rubbed into the meadow there. The most cheering color in all the landscape, shaded with little darker isles of green in the midst of this yellow sea of sedge.

Yet it is the bright and cheerful yellow, as of spring, and with nothing in the least autumnal in it. How this contrasts with the adjacent fields of redtop—now fast falling before the scythe!

AUGUST 2, 1852

The common St. John's wort is now scarce. The reddening sumac berries are of rare beauty. Are they crimson or vermilion? Some sumac leaves where the stem has broken have turned red. Blue-eyed grass lingers still. Is the dodder out of bloom or merely budded? It is a new era with the flowers when the small purple fringed orchis, as now, is found in shady swamps standing along the brooks. (It appears to be alone of its class. Not to be overlooked, it has so much flower though not so high-colored as the arethusa.)

small purple fringed orchis
(*Platanthera psycodes*)

blue-eyed grass (*Sisyrinchium* spp.)

AUGUST 2, 1854

I am inclined now for a pensive evening walk. Methinks we think of spring mornings and autumn evenings. I go via Hubbard Path. Chelone, say two days.

AUGUST 3, 1856

The whorled utricularia is open all day. . . . *Cornus alternifolia* berries ripe, as I go from Holden Swamp shore to Miles Swamp. They are in open cymes, dull blue somewhat depressed globular, tipped with the persistent styles—yet already as usual mostly fallen. But handsomer far are the pretty (bare) red peduncles and pedicels, like fairy fingers spread. They make a show at a distance of a dozen rods even. Something light and open about this tree, but a sort of witches' tree nonetheless.

AUGUST 4, 1851

Now the hardhack and meadowsweet reign, the former one of our handsomest flowers I think. The mayweed, too, dusty by the roadside, and in the fields I scent the sweet-scented life everlasting which is half expanded. The grass is withered by the drought.

AUGUST 4, 1852

What is that weed somewhat like wormwood and amaranth on the ditch by roadside here? (*Acalypha Virginica,* three-seeded mercury.)

AUGUST 5, 1854

Methinks the river's bank is now in its most interesting condition. On the one hand are the light lofty and widespread umbels of the sium [water parsnip, *Sium suave*], pontederias already past their prime, white lilies perhaps not diminished in number, heartleaf flowers, etc. On the other the *Salix Purshiana* [black willow, *S. nigra*] full-foliaged but apparently already *slightly* crisped and imbrowned or yellowed with heat, the buttonbush in full blossom, and the mikania [climbing hempweed, *Mikania scandens*] now covering it with its somewhat hoary bloom. . . . Now then the river's brim is in perfection after the mikania is in bloom and before the pontederia and pads and the willows are too much imbrowned, and the meadows all shorn. But already *very many* pontederia leaves and pads have turned brown or black. The fall in fact begins with the first heat of July.

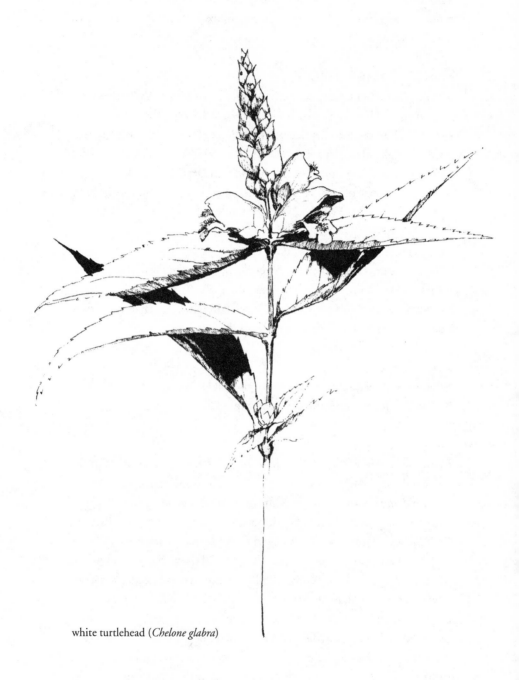

white turtlehead (*Chelone glabra*)

Skunk cabbage, hellebores, convallarias, pontederias, pads, etc., appear to usher it in. It is one long acclivity from winter to midsummer—and another long declivity from midsummer to winter. . . .

I see very few whorled or common utricularias—but the purple ones are exceedingly abundant on both sides the river apparently from one end to the other. The broad pad field on the southwest side of Fair Haven is distinctly purpled with them. Their color is peculiarly high for a water plant.

AUGUST 5, 1855

The common small violet lespedeza [wand bush-clover, *Lespedeza violacea*] out—elliptic-leaved, one inch long. The small white spreading polygala twenty rods behind Wyman site, some time. *Very common this year.*

three-seeded mercury (*Acalypha rhomboidea*)

A[t] haunted house site—as at Bittern Cliff grainfield—I see much apparent *Euphorbia maculata* semi-erect in the grass.

AUGUST 5, 1858

It clears up this morning after several cool cloudy and rainy dog days. The wind is westerly and will probably blow us partway back. The river is unusually full for the season and now quite smooth. The pontederia is apparently in its prime. The buttonbush perhaps a little past, the upper halves of its balls in the sun looking brown generally. The late rose is still conspicuous in clumps advanced into the meadow here and there. See the mikania only in one or two places beginning. The white lilies are less abundant than usual perhaps on account of the high water. The water milkweed flower is an interesting red here and there like roses along the shore. The gratiola begins to yellow the shore in some places—and I notice the unobtrusive

buttonbush (*Cephalanthus occidentalis*)

red of dense fields of stachys [hispid hedge-nettle, *S. hispida*] on the flat shores. The sium has begun to lift its umbels of white flowers above most other plants. The purple utricularia tinges the pools in many places, the most common of all its tribe.

The best show of lilies is on the west side of the bay in Cyrus Hosmer's meadow above the willow row. Many of them are not open at 10 o'clock A.M. I notice one with the sepals perfectly spread flat on the water but the petals still held together in a sharp cone being held by the concave slightly hooked points. Touching this with an oar it opens quickly with a spring. . . .

eyebane (*Euphorbia maculata*)

From off Rainbow Rush Shore I pluck a lily more than five inches in diameter. Its sepals and petals are long and slender—narrow (others are often short, broad, and rounded). The thin white edges of the four sepals are as usual or often tinged with red. There are some twenty-five petals in about four rows. Four alternate ones of the outmost row have a reddish or rosaceous line along the middle between the sepals and both the sepals and the outmost row of petals have seven or eight parallel darkish lines from base to tip. As you look down on the lily it is a pure white star centered with yellow—with its short central anthers orange yellow. . . .

Landed at Fair Haven Pond to smell the *Aster macrophyllus* [large-leaved wood-aster, *Eurybia macrophylla*]. It has a slight fragrance *somewhat like* that of the Maine and northern New Hampshire one. Why has it no more in this latitude? When I first plucked it on Webster Stream I did not know but it was some fragrant garden herb. Here I can detect *some faint* relationship only by perseveringly smelling it.

The purple utricularia is *the* flower of the river today—apparently in its prime. It is very abundant, far more than any other utricularia, especially from Fair Haven Pond upward. That peculiar little bay in the pads just below the inlet of the river I will call Purple Utricularia Bay from its prevalence there. I count a dozen within a square foot, one or two inches above the water, and they tinge the pads with purple for more than a dozen rods. I can distinguish their color thus far. The buds are the darkest or deepest purple. Methinks it is more abundant than usual this year.

AUGUST 6, 1852

Milkweeds and trumpet flowers are important now to contrast with the cool dark shaded sides and recesses of moist copses. I see their red under the willows and alders everywhere against a dark ground. Methinks that blue next to red attracts us in a flower. Blue vervain is now very attractive to me. And then there is that interesting progressive history in its rising ring of blossoms. It has a story. Next to our blood is our prospect of heaven. Does not the blood in fact show blue in the covered veins and arteries—when distance lends enchantment to the view? The sight of it is more affecting than I can describe or account for. . . .

Methinks there are few new flowers of late. An abundance of small fruits takes their place. Summer gets to be an old story. . . .

The weeds are now very high and rank in moist woodpaths, and along such streams as this. I love to follow up the course of the brook and see the cardinal flowers which stand in its midst above the rocks—their brilliant scarlet the more interesting in this open but dark cellar-like wood. The small purple fringed orchises with long dense spikes—all flower—for that is often all that is seen above the leaves of other plants. Is not this the last flower of this peculiar *flower* kind (i.e. all flower and color—the leaves subordinated)? And the *Mimulus ringens* abundant and handsome in these low and rather shady places. Many flowers, of course, like the last are prominent, if you visit such scenes as this—though one who confines himself to the road may never see them.

AUGUST 6, 1853

I see the sunflower's broad disk now in gardens probably a few days—a true sun among flowers. Monarch of August. Do not the flowers of August and September generally resemble suns and stars (sunflowers and asters and the single flowers of the goldenrod)? I once saw one as big as a milk pan in which a mouse had its nest.

AUGUST 6, 1855

The *Ludwigia sphaerocarpus* [round-pod water-primrose, *L. sphaerocarpa*] out maybe a week. I was obliged to wade to it all the way from the shore, the meadow grass cutting my feet above and making them smart. You must have boots here.

The lespedeza with short heads—how long? These great meadows through which I wade have a great abundance of hedge hyssop now in bloom in the water. Small St. John's worts and elodeas, lanceolate loosestrife, arrowheads, small climbing bellflower, also horsemint on the drier clods. These all over the meadow.

AUGUST 7, 1853

The tall buttercup lingers still and the houstonia, not to mention the marsh speedwell and the slender bellflower. . . .

I see the leaves of the two smallest johnsworts reddening. The common johnswort is quite abundant this year and still yellows the fields. I see everywhere in sandy fields the bluecurls knocked off by the rain strewing the ground. As I was walking along a hillside the other day, I smelled pennyroyal—but it was only after a considerable search that I discovered

Allegheny monkeyflower (*Mimulus ringens*)

a single minute plant which I had trodden on, the only one near. When yesterday a boy spilled his huckleberries in the pasture, I saw that Nature was making use of him to disperse her berries, and I might have advised him to pick another dishful. The three kinds of epilobium grow rankly where Hubbard burned his swamp this year, also erechthites. I think that I have observed that this last is a true *fireweed*.

Is it not as language that all natural objects affect the poet? He sees a flower or other object and it is beautiful or affecting to him because it is a symbol of his thought—and what he indistinctly feels or perceives is matured in some other organization. The objects I behold correspond to my mood.

AUGUST 7, 1854

Liatris [Northern blazing-star, *L. scariosa*]. Still autumnal—breezy with a cool vein in the wind—so that, passing from the cool and breezy into the sunny and warm places you begin to love the heat of summer. It is the contrast of the cool wind with the warm sun. I walk over the pinweed field. It is just cool enough in my thin clothes. There is a light on the earth and leaves as if they were burnished. It is the glistening autumnal side of summer. I feel a cool vein in the breeze, which braces my thought, and I pass with pleasure over sheltered and sunny portions of the sand where the summer's heat is undiminished, and I realize what a friend I am losing. . . . This off side of summer glistens like a burnished shield. . . . Tansy is apparently now in its prime and the early goldenrods have acquired a brighter yellow.

AUGUST 8, 1852

I notice now along the North River horsemint, arrowhead, cardinal flower, trumpetweed just coming out. Water parsnip, skullcap (*lateriflora*), monkeyflower, etc., etc. . . . No man ever makes a discovery, ever an observation of the least importance, but he is advertised of the fact by a joy that surprises him. The powers thus celebrate all discovery. The squirrels are now devouring the hazelnuts fast. A lupine blossomed again.

AUGUST 8, 1855

Bluecurls how long? Not long.

AUGUST 8, 1858

You see now in the meadows where the mower's scythe has cut in two the great oval and already black fruit of the skunk cabbage, rough as a nutmeg grater, exposing its numerous nuts. I had quite forgotten the promise of this earliest spring flower which deep in the grass which has sprung up around it, its own leaves for the most part decayed, unremembered by us has been steadily maturing its fruit. How far we have wandered in our thoughts at least since we heard the bee humming in its spathe! I can hardly recall or believe now that for every such black and rather unsightly (?) capsule there was a pretty freckled horn which attracted our attention in the spring. However, most of them lie so low that they escape or are not touched by the scythe. (My friends can rarely guess what fruit it is, but think of pineapples and the like. After lying in the house a week and being wilted and softened, on breaking it open it has an agreeable sweetish scent perchance like a banana, and suggests that it may be edible. But a long while after slightly tasting it, it bites my palate.) . . .

golden hedge-hyssop (*Gratiola aurea*)

I find at Ledum Swamp near the pool the white fringed orchis quite abundant but *past prime,* only a few yet quite fresh. It seems to belong to this sphagnous swamp and is some fifteen to twenty inches high—quite conspicuous, its white spike amid the prevailing green. The leaves are narrow, half folded and almost insignificant. It loves then these cold bogs.

pilewort (fireweed, *Erechtites hieraciifolius*)

How fatally the season is advanced toward the fall! I am not surprised now to see the small rough sunflower. There is much yellow beside now in the fields. How beautiful now the early goldenrods, *Solidago stricta* [*S. juncea*], rising above the wiry grass of the Great Fields in front of Peter's where I sit (which is not worth cutting), not solid yellow like the sunflower, but little pyramidal or sheaf-like golden clouds or mists supported by almost invisible leafy columns, which wave in the wind, like those elms which run

arrowhead (*Sagittaria latifolia*)

mad-dog skullcap (*Scutellaria lateriflora*)

up very tall and slender without a branch and fall over like a sheaf on every side! They give a very indefinite but rich mellow and golden aspect to the field. They are the more agreeable for the indistinctness of their outline, these pillars of fire, clouds which glow only on one side.

AUGUST 10, 1853

Find the *Arabis Canadensis* [*Boechera canadensis*] or sicklepod on Heywood Peak, nearly out of bloom. Never saw it before. New plants spring up where old woods are cut off, having formerly grown here perchance. Many such rarer plants flourish for a few years in such places before they are smothered.

AUGUST 10, 1854

On the southwest side of Conant's Orchard Grove, saw from twenty rods off some patches of purple grass . . . which painted a stripe of hillside next the woods for half a dozen rods in length. It was as high-colored and interesting though not so bright as the patches of rhexia. On examination I found it to be a kind of grass a little less than a foot high with but few green blades and a fine spreading purple top in seed—but close at hand it was but a dull purple and made but little impression on the eye, was even difficult to detect where thin. But viewed in a favorable light fifteen rods off, it was of a fine lively purple color enriching the earth very much.

AUGUST 10, 1858

I see many tobacco pipes—now perhaps in their prime, if not a little late—and hear of pinesap. The Indian pipes, though coming with the fungi and suggesting no doubt a close relation to them (a sort of connecting link between flowers and fungi) is a very interesting flower and will bear a close inspection when fresh. The whole plant has a sweetish earthy odor—though Gray says it is inodorous. I see them now on the leafy floor of this oak wood in families of twelve to thirty sisters of various heights (from two to eight inches) as close together as they can stand. The youngest standing close up to the others. All with faces yet modestly turned downwards under their long hoods. Here is a family of about twenty-five within a diameter of little more than two inches, lifting the dry leaves which elevated around may serve to prop them. Springing up in the shade with so little color, they look the more fragile and delicate. They have very delicate pinkish half-naked stems with a few semitransparent crystalline white scales for leaves—and from the sinuses at the base of the petals without (when their heads are drooping) more or less dark purple is reflected, like the purple of the arteries seen on a nude body.

AUGUST 10, 1860

Juncus paradoxus, that large and late juncus (tailed) as in Hubbard's Close and on island above monument and in Great Meadows—say ten days.

AUGUST 11, 1852

What is that tall plant budded by the Corner Spring? (*Chelone glabra.*) . . . *Aster corymbosus,* path beyond Corner Spring and in Miles Swamp.

Evening draws on while I am gathering bundles of pennyroyal on the further Conantum height. I find it amid the stubble mixed with bluecurls and as fast as I get my hand full tie it into a fragrant bundle. Evening draws on, smoothing the waters and lengthening the shadows now half an hour or more before sundown. What constitutes the charm of this hour of the day? Is it the condensing of dews in the air just beginning, or the grateful increase of shadows in the landscape?

Indian pipe (*Monotropa uniflora*)

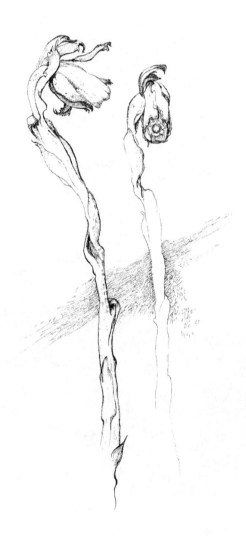

I go along plum path behind Adolphus Clark's. This is a peculiar locality for plants. The *Desmodium Canadense* [showy tick-trefoil] is now apparently in its prime there and very common—with its rather rich spikes of purple flowers. The most (?) conspicuous of the desmodiums. It might be called Desmodium Path. Also the small rough sunflower (now abundant) and the common apocynum (also in bloom as well as going and gone to seed) are very common.

marsh rush (*Juncus paradoxus=J. canadensis*)

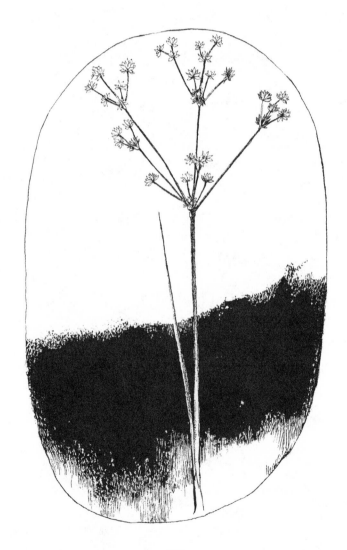

AUGUST 12, 1856

The *Aster patens* [late purple aster, *Symphyotrichum patens*] is very handsome by the side of Moore's Swamp on the bank. Large flowers, more or
less purplish or violet, each commonly (four or five) at the end of a long
peduncle three to six inches long—at right angles with the stem giving it
an open look. Snakehead, or chelone. . . .

white wood aster (*Aster corymbosus=Eurybia divaricata*)

Saw the primrose open at sundown—the corolla suddenly burst part-way open and unfolded rapidly. The sepals flew back with a smart spring. In a minute or two the corolla was opened flat and seemed to rejoice in the cool serene light and air.

AUGUST 12, 1858
That very handsome high-colored fine purple grass grows particularly in dry and rather unproductive soil just above the edge of the meadows on the base of the hills where the hayer does not deign to swing his scythe. He carefully gets the meadow hay and the richer grass that borders it—but leaves this fine purple mist for the walker's harvest.

spreading dogbane (*Apocynum androsaemifolium*)

AUGUST 13, 1853

Hibiscus just beginning to open its large cylindrical buds, as long as your finger, fast unrolling. They look like loosely rolled pink cigars.

AUGUST 13, 1856

Is there not now a prevalence of aromatic herbs in prime? The polygala roots, bluecurls, wormwood, pennyroyal, *Solidago odora* [sweet goldenrod], rough sunflowers, horsemint, etc., etc. Does not the season require this tonic?

swamp rose mallow (*Hibiscus moscheutos*)

AUGUST 14, 1854

3 P.M.—To climbing fern with E. Hoar.

It takes a good deal of care and patience to unwind this fern without injuring it. Sometimes same frond is half leaf, half fruit. E. talked of sending one such leaf to G. Bradford to remind him that the sun still shone in America.

AUGUST 14, 1858

There is brought me this afternoon a *Thalictrum cornuti*—of which the club-shaped filaments (and sepals?) and seed vessels are a bright purple and quite showy.

AUGUST 15, 1851

Hypericum Canadense, Canadian St. John's wort, distinguished by its red capsules. The petals shine under the microscope as if they had a golden dew on them.

Cnicus pumilus [Cirsium pumilum], pasture thistle. How many insects a single one attracts. While you sit by it bee after bee will visit it and busy himself probing for honey and loading himself with pollen regardless of your overshadowing presence. He sees its purple flower from afar, and that use there is in its color.

Oxalis stricta, upright woodsorrel, the little yellow ternate-leaved flower in pastures and cornfields.

Impatiens, noli-me-tangere, or touch-me-not with its dangling yellow pitchers or horns of plenty, which I have seen for a month by damp causeway thickets but the whole plant was so tender and drooped so soon I could not get it home.

AUGUST 15, 1854

The buttonbush is now nearly altogether out of bloom, so that it is too late to see the river's brink in its perfection. It must be seen between the blooming of the mikania and the going out of bloom of the buttonbush. Before you feel this sense of lateness in the year, before the meadows are shorn and the grass of hills and pastures is thus withered and russet.

narrow-leaved St. John's-wort (Canada St. John's-wort, *Hypericum canadense*)

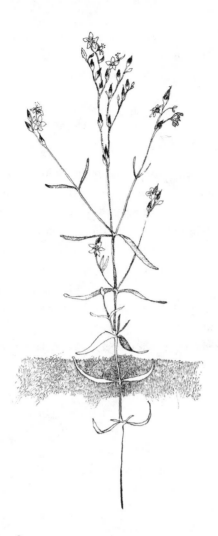

AUGUST 16, 1852

Hibiscus Moscheutos (?), marsh hibiscus apparently N. Barrett's. Perchance
has been out a week. I think it must be the most conspicuous and showy
and at the same time *rich*-colored flower of this month. It is not so conspicuous as the sunflower but of a rarer color — "pale rose-purple" they call
it — like a hollyhock. It is surprising for its amount of color — and seen unexpectedly amid the willows and buttonbushes with the mikania twining
around its stem, you can hardly believe it is a flower. So large and tender it
looks, like the greatest effort of the season to adorn the August days, and
reminded me of that great tender moth the *Actias luna,* which I found on
the water near where it grows. . . .

Galeopsis Tetrahit, common hemp nettle, in roadside by Keyes'. How long? Flower like hedge nettle.

AUGUST 16, 1854
To climbing fern with John Russell.

AUGUST 16, 1856
Cynoglossum officinale [common houndstongue] a long time, mostly gone to seed, at Bull's Path and north roadside below Leppleman's. Its great radical leaves made me think of smooth mullein. The flower has a very peculiar rather sickening odor—Sophia thought like a warm apple pie just from the oven (I did not perceive this). A pretty flower however. I thoughtlessly put a handful of the nutlets into my pocket with my handkerchief. But it took me a long time to pick them out [of] my handkerchief when I got home—and I pulled out many threads in the process. . . .

Amphicarpaea [hog peanut, *A. bracteata*] some time, pods seven eighths of an inch long. *Mimulus ringens* four feet high—and chelone six feet high!

yellow wood-sorrel (*Oxalis stricta*)

jewelweed (touch-me-not, *Impatiens capensis*)

AUGUST 16, 1858

I am surprised to find that where of late years there have been so many cardinal flowers, there are now very few. So much does a plant fluctuate from season to season. Here I found nearly white ones, rare. Channing tells me that he saw a white bobolink in a large flock of them today. Almost all flowers and animals may be found white. As in a large number of cardinal flowers you may find a white one, so in a large flock of bobolinks also, it seems, you may find a white one.

AUGUST 17, 1851

I am not so poor: I can smell the ripening apples. The very rills are deep. The autumnal flowers, the *Trichostema dichotomum*—not only its bright blue flower above the sand but its strong wormwood scent which belongs to the season—feed my spirit, endear the earth to me, make me value my-

179

self and rejoice. The quivering of pigeons' wings reminds me of the tough fiber of the air which they rend.

AUGUST 17, 1852

Is not the hibiscus a very bright pink or even flesh color? It is so delicate and peculiar. I do not think of any flower just like it. It reminds me of some of the wild geraniums most. It is a singular large delicate high-colored flower with a tree-like leaf.

AUGUST 17, 1856

P.M. Walked with Minot Pratt behind his house. . . . Pratt describes finding one or two small yellowish plants on the edge of his field under the hill— like a polygala but twice as large, stiff and points of the flowers turned brown. Leaf cloverlike, three foliate.

AUGUST 18, 1852

The hibiscus flowers are seen a quarter of a mile off over the water, like large roses, now that these high colors are rather rare. Some are exceedingly delicate and pale, almost white, just rose-tinted, others a brighter pink or rose color, and all slightly plaited (the five large petals) and turned toward the sun now in the west, trembling in the wind. So much color looks very rich in these localities. The flowers are some four inches in diameter, as large as water lilies, rising amid and above the buttonbushes and willows, with a large light green tree-like leaf and a stem half an inch in diameter, apparently dying down to a perennial (?) root each year. A superb flower.

AUGUST 18, 1853

What means this sense of lateness that so comes over one now—as if the rest of the year were downhill, and if we had not performed anything before, we should not now. The season of flowers or of promise may be said to be over, and now is the season of fruits—but where is our fruit? The night of the year is approaching. What have we done with our talent? All nature prompts and reproves us. How early in the year it begins to be late. The sound of the crickets even in the spring makes our hearts beat with its awful reproof, while it encourages with its seasonable warning. It matters not by how little we have fallen behind—it seems irretrievably late. The year is full of warnings of its shortness, as is life. The sound of so many in-

common hemp nettle (*Galeopsis tetrahit=G. bifida*)

sects and the sight of so many flowers affect us so. The creak of the cricket
and the sight of the prunella and autumnal dandelion. They say, for the
night cometh in which no man may work.

AUGUST 19, 1851

By the Marlborough road I notice the richly veined leaves of the *Neottia
pubescens* or veined neottia, rattlesnake plantain. I like this last name very
well though it might not be easy to convince a quibbler or proser of its fitness. We want some name to express the mystic wildness of its rich leaves.
Such work as men imitate in their embroidery—unaccountably agreeable
to the eye, as if it answered its end only when it met the eye of man. A reticulated leaf, visible only on one side.

AUGUST 19, 1852

I perceive the fragrance of the clethra on the meadow gales. The checkerberries are in bloom, looking almost like snow-white berries. . . . The trillium berries, six-sided, one inch in diameter, varnished, glossy red, crystal-

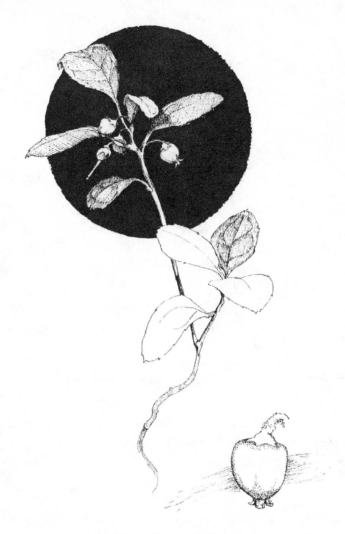

checkerberry (wintergreen, *Gaultheria procumbens*)

line and ingrained, concealed under its green leaves in shady swamps. It is already fall in some of these shady springy swamps as at the Corner Spring. The skunk cabbages and the trilliums, both leaves and fruit, are many flat prostrate, the former decaying and all looking as if early frosts had prevailed. Here too the bright scarlet berries of the arum perhaps premature.

Here is a little brook of very cold spring water, rising a few rods distant with a gray sandy and pebbly bottom, flowing through this dense swampy thicket—where nevertheless the sun falls in here and there between the leaves and shines on its bottom—meandering exceedingly, and sometimes running underground. The trilliums on its bank have fallen into it and bathe their red berries in the water, waving in the stream.

AUGUST 19, 1853

It is a glorious and ever-memorable day. We observe attentively the first beautiful days in the spring, but not so much in the autumn. . . . This day itself has been the great phenomenon—but will it be reported in any journal? As the storm is, and the heat? It is like a great and beautiful flower unnamed.

AUGUST 19, 1856

Dog-day weather as for clouds—but less smoky than before the rains of ten days ago. I see *Hypericum Canadense* and *mutilum* abundantly open at 3 P.M. Apparently they did not bear the dry hot weather of July so well. They are apparently now in prime—but the *Sarothra* [pineweed, *Hypericum gentianoides*] is not open at this hour. The *perforatum* is quite scarce now, and apparently the *corymbosum* [spotted St. John's-wort, *H. punctatum*]—the *ellipticum* quite done. The small hypericums have a peculiar smart somewhat lemon-like fragrance, but bee-like. . . .

The whorled polygala is a plant almost universally dispersed but inconspicuous.

AUGUST 20, 1851

The *Lobelia inflata,* Indian tobacco, meets me at every turn. At first I suspect some new bluish flower in the grass, but stooping see the inflated pods. Tasting one such herb convinces me that there *are* such things as drugs which may either kill or cure. (A farmer tells me that he knows when his horse has eaten it, because it makes him slobber badly.)

In the dry ditch near Abel Minott's house that was I see cardinal flowers, with their red artillery, reminding me of soldiers—red men, war, and bloodshed. Some are four and a half feet high.

Thy sins shall be as scarlet. Is it my sins that I see? It shows how far a little color can go, for the flower is not large, yet it makes itself seen from afar, and so answers the purpose for which it was colored completely.

common St. John's-wort (*Hypericum perforatum*)

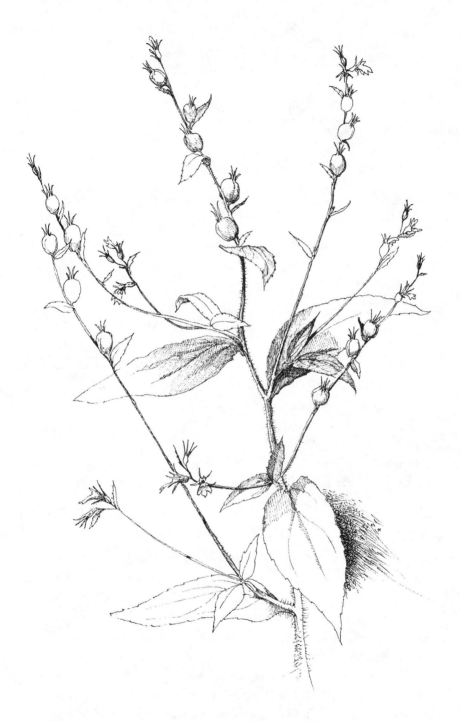

Indian tobacco (*Lobelia inflata*)

flat-topped goldenrod (spear-leaved goldenrod,
Solidago lanceolata=Euthamia graminifolia)

AUGUST 20, 1857

The hillside at Clintonia Swamp is in some parts quite shingled with the
rattlesnake plantain (*Goodyera pubescens*) leaves overlapping one another.
The flower is now apparently in its prime.

AUGUST 21, 1851

It is remarkable that animals are often obviously manifestly related to the
plants which they feed upon or live among—as caterpillars, butterflies,
tree toads, partridges, chewinks—and this afternoon I noticed a yellow
spider on a goldenrod. As if every condition might have its expression in
some form of animated being. Spear-leaved goldenrod in path to northeast of Flint's Pond.

Hieracium paniculatum, a very delicate and slender hawkweed. I have
now found all the hawkweeds. Singular these genera of plants—plants
manifestly related yet distinct. They suggest a history to Nature—a natural *history* in a new sense.

The grass-poly by the Lincoln road with its "fine purple" flowers. *Decodon verticillatus,* swamp loosestrife. Those in the water do not generally blossom. What stout woody perennial root stocks. It is a handsome purple flower falling over wreath-like on every side with an epilobium look—a *lively* purple. . . .

This coloring and reddening of the leaves toward fall is interesting, as if the sun had so prevailed that even the leaves better late than never were turning to flowers—so filled with mature juices, the whole plant turns at length to one flower and all its leaves are petals around its fruit or dry seed. A second flowering to celebrate the maturity of the fruit.

panicled hawkweed (*Hieracium paniculatum*)

Brought home a great *Eupatorium purpureum* [Eastern or coastal plain Joe-Pye weed, *Eutrochium dubium*] from Miles' Swamp (made species *fistulosum* by Barratt). It is ten and a half feet high and one inch in diameter, said to grow to twelve feet. The corymb eighteen and a half inches wide by fifteen inches deep, the largest leaves thirteen by three inches. The stem hollow throughout. This I found to my surprise when I undertook to make a flute of it trusting it was closed at the leaves, but there is no more pith there than elsewhere. It would serve many purposes as a water pipe, etc. Probably the Indians knew and used it. They might have blowed arrows through a straight one. It would yield an available hollow tube six feet long.

swamp loosestrife
(*Decodon verticillatus*)

AUGUST 21, 1858

How yellow that kind of hedgehog (?) sedge in the toad pool by Cyrus Hubbard's corner. (*Cyperus phymatodes.*)

AUGUST 22, 1852

Just smelled an apple which carried me forward to those days when they will be heaped in the orchards and about the cider mills. The fragrance of some fruits is not to be forgotten along with that of flowers. Is not the high blackberry our finest berry? I gather very sweet ones which weigh down the vines in sproutlands.

AUGUST 22, 1858

The *cyperus* (*phymatodes,* etc.) now yellows edges of pools and half-bare low grounds.

AUGUST 22, 1859

The circles of the blue vervain flowers, now risen near to the top, show how far advanced the season is.

yellow nut-grass (*Cyperus phymatodes=C. esculentus*)

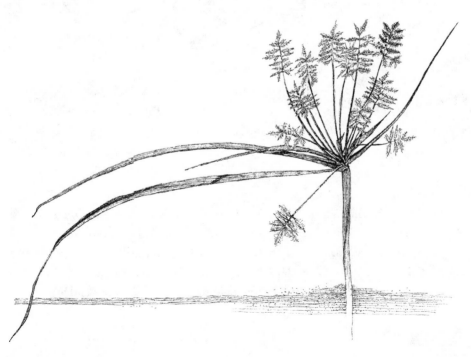

The ferns in low shady woods are faded. *Hydrocotyle Americana,* marsh
pennywort, by the Lee place path. It probably opened in June or July. Saw
a new form of arrowhead leaf with linear lobes, but the flowers apparently
the same, a crystalline white. The bank at the bathing place has now a new
kind of beauty. It is spotted with bright scarlet cardinal flowers and bright
purple vernonias.

water pennywort (*Hydrocotyle americana*)

AUGUST 23, 1853

Potato fields are full of Roman wormwood now. I am braced and encouraged by the rank growth of this aromatic plant concealing the potato vines which are already nearly half-decayed. . . .

The *Solidago nemoralis* [gray goldenrod] now yellows the dry fields with its recurved standard a little more than a foot high—marching to the Holy Land, a countless host of crusaders.

AUGUST 23, 1856

On the west side of Emerson's Cliff I notice many *Gerardia pedicularia* [fern-leaved false foxglove, *Aureolaria pedicularia*] out. A bee is hovering about one bush. The flowers are not yet open—and if they were, perhaps he could not enter. He proceeds at once head downward to the base of the tube—and extracts the sweet there and departs.

Examining I find that every flower has a small hole pierced through the tube, commonly through calyx and all, opposite the nectary. This does not hinder its opening. The Rape of the Flower! The bee knew where the sweet lay and was unscrupulous in his mode of obtaining it. A certain violence tolerated by nature.

AUGUST 23, 1858

The *rhexia* in the field west of Clintonia Swamp makes a great show now though a little past prime. I go through the swamp wading through the luxuriant cinnamon fern which has complete possession of the swamp floor. Its great fronds curving this way and that remind me [of] a tropical vegetation. . . .

See an abundance of pinesap on the right of Pinesap Path. It is almost all erect, some eight to nine inches high, and all *effete* there. Some stems are reddish. It lifts the leaves with it like the Indian pipe—but is not so delicate as that. The Indian pipe is still pushing up.

AUGUST 24, 1851

The interregnum in the blossoming of flowers being *well* over, many small flowers blossom now in the low grounds having just reached their summer. It is now dry enough, and they feel the heat their tenderness required. The autumnal flowers—goldenrods, asters, and johnswort—though they have made demonstrations have not yet commenced to reign. The tansy is already getting stale. It is perhaps the first conspicuous yellow flower that passes from the stage. . . .

Did I find the dwarf tree primrose in Hubbard's meadow today? *Stachys aspera,* hedge nettle or woundwort, a rather handsome purplish flower.

AUGUST 24, 1852

Surely the high blackberry is the finest berry—not by dusty roadsides, but when now the season is rather late, and you find them in some rocky sproutland, far from any road, fully ripe, having escaped the pickers— weighing down their stems and half hidden amid the green leaves of other plants, black and shiny, ready to drop with a spirited juice. . . . In R.W.E.'s garden, *Pilea pumila,* richweed, August, and *Sonchus oleraceus,* common sow thistle with a small dandelion-like flower—and also *Amaranthus albus* [prostrate pigweed], the last July (?).

common hedge-nettle (*Stachys tenuifolia*)

AUGUST 25, 1851

Checkerberry in bloom. Blue-eyed grass still.

clearweed (*Pilea pumila*)

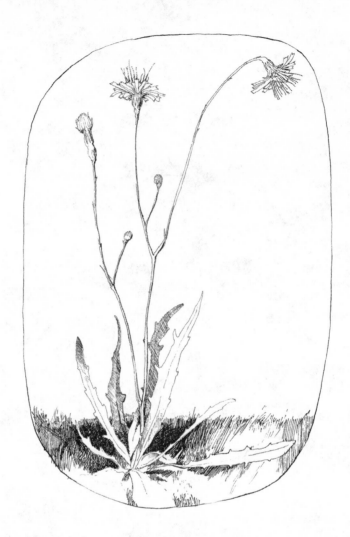

AUGUST 25, 1858

Cyperus strigosus [straw-colored flatsedge] under Clamshell Hill—that yellowish fuzzy-headed plant five to twelve inches high now apparently in prime. Also in Mrs. Hoar's garden. Also *Cyperus phymatodes,* very much like last, in Mrs. Hoar's garden, which has little tubers at a distance from the base, apparently in prime.

AUGUST 26, 1853

The fall dandelion is as conspicuous and abundant now in Tuttle's meadow as buttercups in the spring. It takes their place. Saw the comet in the west tonight. It made me think of those imperfect white seeds in a watermelon—an immature ineffectual meteor.

fall dandelion (*Scorzoneroides autumnalis*)

Two interesting tall purplish grasses appear to be the prevailing ones now in dry and sterile neglected fields and hillsides—*Andropogon furcatus,* forked beard grass [big bluestem, *A. gerardii*], and apparently *Andropogon scoparius,* purple wood grass [little bluestem, *Schizachyrium scoparium*] (though the last appears to have three awns like an *Aristida*).

The first is a very tall and slender-culmed grass, with four or five purple finger-like spikes raying upward from the top. It is very abundant on the hillside behind Peter's.

The other is quite slender, two to three or four feet high, growing in tufts and somewhat curving, also commonly purple and with pretty purple stigmas like the last—and it has purple anthers. When out of bloom its appressed spikes are recurving and have a whitish hairy or fuzzy look.

These are the prevailing conspicuous flowers where I walk this afternoon in dry ground. I have sympathy with them because they are despised by the farmer—and occupy sterile and neglected soil. They also by their rich purple reflections or tinges seem to express the ripeness of the year. It is high-colored like ripe grapes—and expresses a maturity which the spring did not suggest. Only the August sun could have thus burnished these culms and leaves.

The farmer has long since done his upland haying—and he will not deign to bring his scythe to where these slender wild grasses have at length flowered thinly. You often see the bare sand between them. I walk encouraged between the tufts of purple wood grass—over the sandy fields by the shrub oaks, glad to recognize these simple contemporaries. These two are almost the first grasses that I have learned to distinguish. I did not know by how many friends I was surrounded. The purple of their culms excites me like that of the pokeweed stems. . . .

Each humblest plant or weed, as we call it, stands there to express some thought or mood of ours—and yet how long it stands in vain! I have walked these Great Fields so many Augusts and never yet distinctly recognized these purple companions that I have there. I have brushed against them and trampled them down, forsooth—and now at last they have, as it were, risen up and blessed me.

The *Medeola Virginica,* cucumber root, the whorl-leaved plant, is now in green fruit.

Goodyera pubescens, rattlesnake plantain, is apparently a *little* past its prime. It is very abundant on Clintonia Swamp hillside, quite erect with its white spike eight to ten inches high on the sloping hillside, the lower half or more turning brown—but the beautifully reticulated leaves which pave the moist shady hillside about its base are the chief attraction. These oval leaves, perfectly smooth like velvet to the touch, about one inch long, have

Indian cucumber root (*Medeola virginiana*)

a broad white midrib and four to six longitudinal white veins very prettily and thickly connected by other conspicuous white veins transversely—and irregularly—all on a dark rich green ground. Is it not the prettiest leaf that paves the forest floor? . . .

The cardinals in the ditch make a splendid show now though they would have been much fresher and finer a week ago. They nearly fill the ditch for thirty-five rods perfectly straight, about three feet high. I count at random ten in one square foot—and as they are two feet wide by thirty-five rods there are four or five thousand at least, and maybe more. They look like slender plumes of soldiers advancing—in a dense troop—and a few white (or rather pale pink) ones are mingled with the scarlet. That is the most splendid show of cardinal flowers I ever saw.

AUGUST 27, 1859
I often see yarrow with a delicate pink tint—very distinct from the common pure white ones.

AUGUST 28, 1852
Sicyos angulatus, one-seeded star cucumber in Aunt's garden probably in July. *Nepeta Glechoma*, ground ivy or gill probably May, now out of bloom. . . . The sweet viburnum not yet purple and the maple-leaved still yellowish. Hemp still in blossom.

AUGUST 28, 1856
Now the black cherries in sproutlands are in their prime—and the black chokeberries just after huckleberries and blueberries. They are both very abundant this year. The branches droop with cherries.

AUGUST 28, 1859
The flowers I see at present are autumn flowers—such as have risen above the stubble in shorn fields since it was cut, whose tops have commonly been clipped by the scythe or the cow—or the late flowers, as asters and goldenrods which grow in neglected fields and along ditches and hedgerows.

AUGUST 29, 1856
The *Helianthus decapetalus* apparently a variety—with eight petals about three feet high, leaves petioled but not wing-petioled. Broader-leaved than

bur cucumber (*Sicyos angulatus*)

that of August 12th, quite ovate with a tapering point, with ciliate petioles, thin but quite rough beneath and above, stem purple and smoothish. Hosmer's bank, opposite Azalea Swamp. Fragrant everlasting in prime and very abundant whitening Carter's pasture. Ribwort still. An apparent white vervain with bluish flowers—as blue as bluets even or more so— roadside beyond Farmer's barn.

AUGUST 29, 1857

Gerardia tenuifolia—a new plant to Concord[10] apparently in prime—at entrance to Owl Nest Path and generally in that neighborhood. (Also on Conantum height above orchard, two or three days later.) This species grows on dry ground, or higher than the purpurea, and is more delicate.

ground ivy (gill-over-the-ground, *Nepeta glechoma=Glechoma hederacea*)

The vernonia is one of the most conspicuous flowers now where it grows—
a very rich color. It is somewhat past its prime—perhaps about with the
red eupatorium.

AUGUST 30, 1851

Saturday. I perceive in the Norway cinquefoil, *Potentilla Norvegica* [rough
cinquefoil], now nearly out of blossom, that the alternate five leaves of
the calyx are closing over the seeds to protect them. This evidence of fore-
thought, this simple *reflection* in a double sense of the term, in this flower
is affecting to me. . . . There is one door closed, of the closing year. Nature
ordered this bending back of the calyx leaves, and every year since this

plant was created her order has been faithfully obeyed. And this plant acts not an obscure but essential part in the revolution of the seasons. I am not ashamed to be contemporary with the Norway cinquefoil. May I perform my part as well! There is so much done toward closing up the year's accounts. It is as good as if I saw the great globe go round. It is as if I saw the Janus doors of the year closing.

AUGUST 30, 1853

As I went along from the Minott house to the Bidens Brook I was quite bewildered by the beauty and variety of the asters now in their prime there. . . . Why so many asters and goldenrods now? The sun has shone on the earth, and the goldenrod is his fruit. The stars too have shone on it and the asters are their fruit.

The purple balls of the carrion flower now open a little beneath, standing out on all sides six or eight inches from the twining stem, are very handsome. They are covered with a blue bloom and when this is rubbed off by leaves are a shining blackish.

AUGUST 30, 1854

The *Bidens frondosa,* some time—distinguished by its being fairly pinnate, with from three to five leafets.

AUGUST 30, 1856

I saw bags of cranberries just gathered and tied up, on the banks of Beck Stow's Swamp. They must have been raked out of the water, now so high, before they should rot. I left my shoes and stockings on the bank far off— and waded barelegged through rigid andromeda and other bushes a long way to the soft open sphagnous center of the swamp. . . .

I seemed to have reached a new world—so wild a place that the very huckleberries grew hairy and were inedible. I feel as if I were in Rupert's Land—and a slight cool but agreeable shudder comes over me as if equally far away from human society. What's the need of visiting far-off mountains and bogs if a half-hour's walk will carry me into such wildness and novelty? But why should not as wild plants grow here as in Berkshire—as in Labrador?

thin-leaved sunflower (*Helianthus decapetalus*)

devil's beggar-ticks
(*Bidens frondosa*)

AUGUST 30, 1858

Find at Dodd's shore: *Eleocharis obtusa* [blunt spikerush], some time out of bloom (*fresh* still at Pratt's Pool). Also *Juncus acuminatus* (?) [sharp-fruited rush] just done (also apparently *later* and yet in bloom at Pout's Nest). Also what I called *Juncus scirpoides* but which appears to be *Juncus paradoxus* [*J. canadensis*] with seeds tailed at both ends (it is fresher than what I have seen before and smaller), not done. Some of it with *few flowers!* A terete leaf rises above the flower. It looks like a small bayonet rush.

The *Juncus militaris* [bayonet rush] has been long out of bloom. The leaf is three feet long, the whole plant four or five. It grows on edge of Grindstone Meadow and above. It would look more like a bayonet if the leaf were shorter than the flowering stem, which *last* is the bayonet part. This is my rainbow rush.

AUGUST 30, 1859

The pasture thistle though past its prime is quite common — and almost every flower (i.e. thistle), wherever you meet with it, has one or more bumblebees on it clambering over its mass of florets. One such bee which I disturb has much ado before he can rise from the grass and get under weigh — as if he were too heavily laden — and at last he flies but low. Now that flowers are rarer, almost every one of whatever species has bees or butterflies upon it.

sweet pepperbush
(*Clethra alnifolia*)

AUGUST 31, 1850

The purple flowers of the humble trichostema mingled with the worm-wood, smelling like it.

And the spring-scented, dandelion-scented primrose, yellow primrose.

The swamp pink, *Azalea viscosa* [swamp azalea, *Rhododendron viscosum*]—its now withered pistils standing out. . . .

The alder-leaved clethra (*Clethra alnifolia*), sweet-smelling queen of the swamp—its long white racemes.

We are most apt to remember and cherish the flowers which appear earliest in the spring. I look with equal affection on those which are the latest to bloom in the fall.

AUGUST 31, 1851

What relation does the fall dandelion bear to the spring dandelion? There is a rank scent of tansy now on some roads—disagreeable to many people, from being associated in their minds with funerals where it is sometimes put into the coffin and about the corpse. . . .

Cohush now in fruit, ivory-white berries tipped *now* with black on stout red pedicels—*Actaea alba. Collinsonia Canadensis,* horseweed. I had discovered this singular flower there new to me. And having a botany by me looked it out. What a surprise and disappointment—what an insult and impertinence to my curiosity and expectation—to have given me the name "horseweed." . . .

richweed (horseweed, *Collinsonia canadensis*)

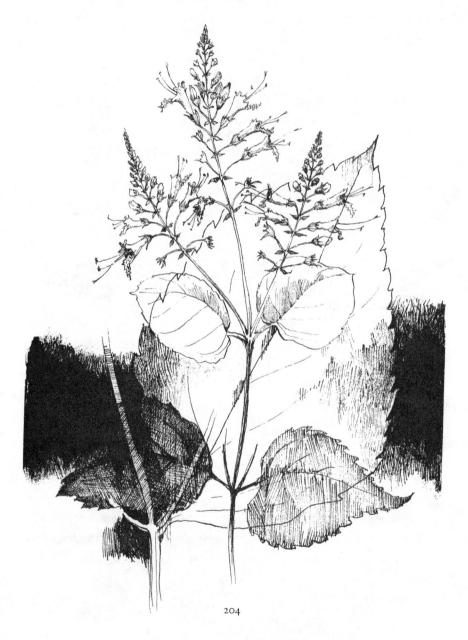

It was the filiform crowfoot, *Ranunculus filiformis,* that I saw by the riverside the other day and today.[11] The flowers of the nettle-leaved vervain are now near the ends of the spikes like the blue. . . .

Utricularia inflata, whorled bladderwort, floating on the water at same place.

AUGUST 31, 1852

Landed near the bee tree. A bumblebee on a cow-wheat blossom sounded like the engine's whistle far over the woods — then like an aeolian harp. . . .

I ramble over the wooded hill on the right beyond the Pantry. The bushy gerardia is now very conspicuous with its great yellow trumpets on hillsides or sproutlands. Sometimes you come upon a large field of them. The buds or closed tubes are as handsome at least as the flowers. . . . *Utricu-*

American cow-wheat (*Melampyrum lineare*)

laria inflata or whorled bladderwort, numerous in Fair Haven Pond. I found it the same day of the month last year.

AUGUST 31, 1853
The asters and goldenrods are now in their prime, I think. The rank growth of flowers (commonly called weeds) in this swamp now impresses me like a harvest of flowers. I am surprised at their luxuriance and profusion. . . . There has been no such rank flowering up to this.

One would think that all the poison that is in the earth and air must be extracted out of them by this rank vegetation.

AUGUST 31, 1859
While I stand under a pine for shelter during the rain on Fair Haven Hillside—I see many sarsaparilla plants fallen and *withering green,* i.e. before changing. It is as if they had a weak hold on the earth in the subterranean stocks.

SEPTEMBER I, 1853
I am struck again and again by the richness of the meadow beauty lingering, though it will last some time in little dense purple patches by the sides of the meadows. It is so low it escapes the scythe. It is not so much distinct flowers (it is so low and dense) but a colored patch on the meadow. Yet how few observe it—how, in one sense, it is wasted. How little thought the mower or the cranberry raker bestows on it. How few girls or boys come to see it!

SEPTEMBER I, 1856
The very dense clusters of the smilacina berries,[12] finely purple-dotted on a pearly ground are very interesting—also the smaller and similar clusters of the two-leaved convallaria. Many of the last and a few of the first are already turned red, clear semilucent red. They have a pleasant sweetish taste.

SEPTEMBER I, 1857
On the west side of Fair Haven Pond, an abundance of the *Utricularia purpurea*—and of the whorled, etc.—whose finely dissected leaves are a rich sight in the water.

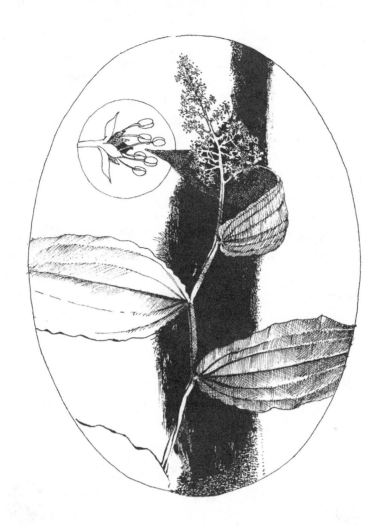

false Solomon's seal (*Smilacina racemosa=Maianthemum racemosum*)

The autumnal dandelion is a prevailing flower now—but since it shuts up in the afternoon it might not be known as common unless you were out in the morning or in a dark afternoon.

Now at 11 A.M. it makes quite a show yet at 2 P.M. I do not *notice* it.

The small cornel or bunchberry is in bloom now (!!) near the pond.

I think we may detect that some sort of preparation and faint expectation preceded every discovery we have made. We blunder into no discovery—but it will appear that we have prayed and disciplined ourselves for it. Some years ago I sought for Indian hemp (*Apocynum cannabinum*) hereabouts in vain—and concluded that it did not grow here. A month or two ago I read again as many times before that its blossoms were very small, scarcely a third as large as those of the common species, and for some unaccountable reason this distinction kept recurring to me—and I regarded the size of the flowers I saw, though I did not believe that it grew here—and in a day or two my eyes fell on [it], aye, in three different places and different varieties of it. Also a short time ago I was satisfied that there was but one kind of sunflower (*divaricatus*) [woodland sunflower, *Helianthus divaricatus*] indigenous here. Hearing that one had found another

kind it occurred to me that I had seen a taller one than usual lately, but not so distinctly did I remember this as to name it to him or even fully remember it myself. (I rather remembered it afterward.) But within that hour my genius conducted me to where I had seen the tall plants—and it was the other man's new kind. The next day I found a third kind miles from there—and a few days after a fourth in another direction.

I commonly observe that I make my most interesting botanical discoveries when I [am] in a thrilled and expectant mood, perhaps wading in some remote swamp where I have just found something novel and feel more than usually remote from the town. Or some rare plant which for some reason has occupied a strangely prominent place in my thoughts— for some time—will present itself. My expectation ripens to discovery. I am prepared for strange things. . . .

Spiranthes cernua, apparently some days at least, though not yet generally—a cool late flower growing with fringed gentian. . . .

There was an old gentleman here today who lived in Concord when he was young and remembers how Dr. Ripley talked to him and other little boys from the pulpit as they came into church with their hands full of lilies—saying that those lilies looked so fresh that they must have been gathered that morning! Therefore he must have committed the sin of bathing this morning!! Why, this is as sacred a river as the Ganges is.

SEPTEMBER 3, 1851
Walk often in drizzly weather for then the small weeds (especially if they stand on bare ground), covered with raindrops like beads, appear more beautiful than ever. The hypericums for instance. They are equally beautiful when covered with dew—fresh and adorned, almost spirited away in a robe of dewdrops. . . .

Identified spotted spurge, *Euphorbia maculata,* apparently out of blossom.

SEPTEMBER 3, 1853
The soapwort gentian out abundantly in Flint's Bridge Lane, apparently for a week—a surprisingly deep *faintly* purplish blue. Crowded bunches of ten or a dozen sessile and closed narrow or oblong diamond or sharp

bunchberry (*Cornus canadensis*)

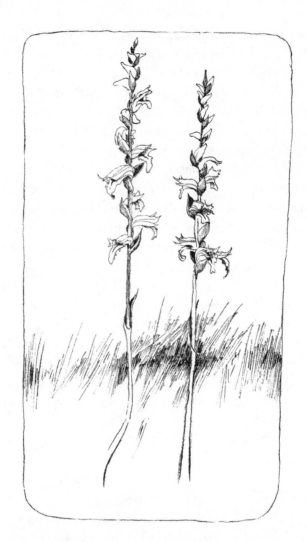

dome-shape flowers. The whole bunch like many sharp domes of an Oriental city crowded together. I have here actually drawn my pen round one. It is the flowering of the sky. The sky has descended and kissed the earth. In (at top) a whorl of clear smooth rich green leaves. Why come these blue flowers thus late in the year? A dome-like crowd of domelets.

SEPTEMBER 4, 1853

Would it not be worth the while to devote one day each year to collecting with pains the different kinds of asters, perhaps about this time—and another to the goldenrods.

nodding ladies'-tresses (*Spiranthes cernua*)

SEPTEMBER 4, 1856

The feverbush is conspicuously flower-budded. Even its spicy leaves have been cut by the tailor bee—and circular pieces taken out. He was perhaps attracted by its smoothness and soundness.

Large puffballs some time.

SEPTEMBER 4, 1859

Three kinds of thistle are *commonly* out now—the *pasture,* lanceolate, and swamp—and on them all you are pretty sure to see one or two humblebees. They become more prominent and interesting in the scarcity of purple flowers. (On many you see also the splendid goldfinch, yellow and black (?) like the humblebee.) The thistles beloved of humblebees and goldfinches.

SEPTEMBER 5, 1852

The petals of the purple gerardia strew the brooks. The oval spikes of somewhat pear-shaped berries of the arum perhaps vermilion color now—

bottle gentian (soapwort gentian, *Gentiana clausa*)

its scapes bent to the ground. These by their color must have caught an Indian's eye. . . .

What is that bidens now just blossomed—rough-stemmed or bristly—with undivided lanceolate serrate and strongly connate leaves, short but conspicuous rays, achenia four-awned and downwardly barbed? (*B. cernua.*)

SEPTEMBER 5, 1854

Saw some buttonbush balls going to seed, which were really quite a *rich red* over a green base, especially in this evening light. They are commonly greener and much duller reddish.

small-flowered gerardia (purple gerardia,
Agalinis purpurea var. *parviflora*)

The ripening grapes begin to fill the air with their fragrance.

The vervain will hardly do for a clock—for I perceive that some later and smaller specimens have not much more than begun to blossom. While most have done. Saw a tall pear tree by the roadside beyond Harris' in front of Hapgood's. Saw the lambkill, *Kalmia angustifolia,* in blossom, a few fresh blossoms at *the ends* of the fresh twigs—on Strawberry Hill. Beautiful bright flowers. . . .

The elecampane, *Inula Helenium,* with its broad leaves wrinkled underneath and the remains of sunflower-like blossoms in front of Nathan Brooks', Acton, and near J. H. Wheeler's.

nodding bur-marigold (*Bidens cernua*)

fox grape (*Vitis labrusca*)

SEPTEMBER 6, 1859

The liatris is perhaps a little past prime. It is a very rich purple in favorable lights—and makes a great show where it grows. Anyone to whom it is new will be surprised to learn that it is a wild plant. For prevalence and effect it may be put with the vernonia [New York ironweed, *V. noveboracensis*]—and it has a general resemblance to thistles and knapweed, but is a handsomer plant than any of them.

SEPTEMBER 7, 1851

The scenery when it is truly seen, reacts on the life of the seer. How to live. How to get the most life! As if you were to teach the young hunter how to entrap his game. How to extract its honey from the flower of the world.

elecampane (*Inula helenium*)

That is my everyday business. I am as busy as a bee about it. I ramble over all fields on that errand and am never so happy as when I feel myself heavy with honey and wax. I am like a bee searching the livelong day for the sweets of nature. Do I not impregnate and intermix the flowers, produce rarer and finer varieties by transferring my eyes from one to another? I do as naturally and as joyfully, with my own humming music, seek honey all the day. With what honeyed thought any experience yields me I take a bee line to my cell. It is with flowers I would deal. . . . The Roman wormwood is beginning to yellow-green my shoes—intermingled with the bluecurls over the sand in this grainfield. Perchance some poet likened this golden dust to the ambrosia of the gods.

SEPTEMBER 7, 1857
Rhus venenata berries are whitening. Its leaves appear very fresh—of a rich dark damp green—and very little eaten by insects.

SEPTEMBER 7, 1858
I turn Anthony's corner. It is an early September afternoon, melting warm and sunny. The thousands of grasshoppers leaping before you reflect gleams of light. A little distance off the field is yellowed with a Xerxean army of *Solidago nemoralis* between me and the sun. The earth song of the cricket comes up through all—and ever and anon the hot *z*-ing of the locust is heard. (Poultry is now fattening on grasshoppers.) The dry deserted fields are one mass of yellow—like a color shoved to one side on Nature's palette. You literally wade in flowers knee deep.

SEPTEMBER 7, 1860
Common rose hips as handsome as ever.

SEPTEMBER 8, 1851
The year may be in its summer, in its manhood, but it is no longer in the flower of its age. It is a season of withering, of dust and heat—a season of small fruits and trivial experiences. Summer thus answers to manhood. But there is an aftermath in early autumn—and some spring flowers bloom again, followed by an Indian summer of finer atmosphere and of a pensive beauty. May my life be not destitute of its Indian summer. A season of fine and clear mild weather in which I may prolong my hunting before the winter comes. When I may once more lie on the ground with

faith as in spring—and even with more serene confidence. And then I will [wrap the] drapery of summer about me and lie down to pleasant dreams. As one year passes into another through the medium of winter—so does this our life pass into another through the medium of death.

SEPTEMBER 8, 1853
Roses, apparently *R. lucida,* abundantly out on a warm bank on Great Fields by Moore's Swamp, with *Viola pedata.*

SEPTEMBER 8, 1854
The witch hazel on Dwarf Sumac Hill looks as if it would begin to blossom in a day or two.

poison sumac (*Rhus venenata=Toxicodendron vernix*)

SEPTEMBER 9, 1850

The thistle is now in bloom, which every child is eager to clutch once. Just a child's handful.

SEPTEMBER 9, 1858

Under the rocks near the slippery elm, the *Gymnostichum hystrix,* bottle-brush grass, hedgehog grass, long done.

SEPTEMBER 10, 1851

The poke is a very rich and striking plant. Some which stand under the Cliffs quite dazzled me with their now purple stems gracefully drooping each way, their rich somewhat yellowish purple-veined leaves, their bright purple racemes . . . flower buds, flowers, ripe berries and dark purple ones,

bottlebrush-grass (*Gymnostichum hystrix=Elymus hystrix*)

and calyx-like petals which have lost their fruit all on the same plant. I love to see any redness in the vegetation of the temperate zone. It is the richest color. I love to press these berries between my fingers and see their rich purple wine staining my hand. It asks a bright sun on it to make it show to best advantage and it must be seen at this season of the year. It speaks to my blood.

pokeweed (*Phytolacca americana*)

SEPTEMBER 11, 1852

How much fresher some flowers look in rainy weather. When I thought they were about done they appear to revive—and moreover their beauty is enhanced as if by the contrast of the louring atmosphere with their bright colors. Such are the purple gerardia and the *Bidens cernua*. The purple gerardia and bluecurls are interesting for their petals strewn about, beaten down by the rain.

SEPTEMBER 11, 1859

This being a cloudy and somewhat rainy day the autumnal dandelion is open in the afternoon.

bluecurls (*Trichostema dichotomum*)

SEPTEMBER 12, 1851

Found a violet, apparently *Viola cucullata* or hood-leaved violet in bloom in Baker's Meadow beyond Pine Hill. Also the *Bidens cernua,* nodding bur-marigold, with five petals—in same place. . . .

When I got into the Lincoln road I perceived a singular sweet scent in the air, which I suspected arose from some plant now in a peculiar state owing to the season, but though I smelled everything around I could not detect it, but the more eagerly I smelled the further I seemed to be from finding it. But when I gave up the search, again it would be wafted to me. It was one of the sweet scents which go to make the autumn air, which fed my sense of smell rarely and dilated my nostrils. I felt the better for it. Methinks that I possess the sense of smell in greater perfection than usual—and have the habit of smelling of every plant I pluck. How autumnal is the scent of ripe grapes now by the roadside!

SEPTEMBER 12, 1853

I was struck this afternoon with the beauty of the *Aster corymbosus* with its corymbed flowers with seven or eight long slender white rays pointed at both ends ready to curl shaving-like and purplish disks. One of the more interesting asters.

SEPTEMBER 12, 1859

The four kinds of bidens (*frondosa, connata, cernua,* and *chrysanthemoides*) abound now, but *much* of the *Beckii* was drowned by the rise of the river. *Omitting this,* the first two are inconspicuous flowers, cheap and ineffectual, commonly without petals (like the erechthites) but the third and fourth are conspicuous and interesting—expressing by their brilliant yellow the ripeness of the low grounds. . . .

I stand in Moore's Swamp and look at Garfield's dry bank—now before the woods *generally* are changed at all. How ruddy ripe that dry hillside by the swamp—covered with goldenrods and clumps of hazel bushes here and there, now more or less scarlet. . . .

Many a dying field now (like that of Sted Buttrick's on the Great Fields) is one dense mass of the bright golden recurved wands of the *Solidago nemoralis* (a *little* past prime) waving in the wind—and turning upward to the light hundreds if not a thousand flowerets each. It is the greatest mass of conspicuous flowers in the year—and uniformly from one to two feet high just rising above the withered grass all over the largest fields, now when pumpkins and other yellow fruits begin to gleam, now before the woods are *noticeably* changed.

SEPTEMBER 13, 1851
The cross-leaved polygala emits its fragrance as if at will. You are quite sure you smelled it and are ravished with its sweet fragrance, but now it has no smell. You must not hold it too near, but hold it on all sides and at all distances, and there will perchance be wafted to you sooner or later a very sweet and penetrating fragrance. What it is like you cannot surely tell, for you do not enjoy it long enough nor in volume enough to compare it. It is very likely that you will not discover any fragrance while you are rudely smelling at it—you can only remember that you once perceived it.

SEPTEMBER 13, 1852
Asters various shades of blue and especially the smaller kinds of *dense-flowering white ones* are more than ever by the roadsides. . . .

How earnestly and rapidly each creature, each flower, is fulfilling its part while its day lasts! Nature never lost a day—nor a moment. As the planet in its orbit and around its axis, so do the seasons, so does time revolve with a rapidity inconceivable. In the moment, in the aeon well employed, time ever advances with this rapidity. To an idler the man employed is terribly rapid. He that is not behind his time is swift. The immortals are swift. Clear the track. The plant that waited a whole year and then blossomed the instant it was ready and the earth was ready for it without the conception of delay, was rapid. To the conscience of the idle man, the stillness of a placid September day sounds like the din and whirl of a factory. Only employment can still this din in the air. . . .

I must walk more with free senses. It is as bad to *study* stars and clouds as flowers and stones. . . . I have the habit of attention to such excess that my senses get no rest—but suffer from a constant strain. Be not preoccupied with looking. Go not to the object. Let it come to you.

When I have found myself ever looking down and confining my gaze to the flowers, I have thought it might be well to get into the habit of observing the clouds as a corrective. But ha! that study would be just as bad. What I need is not to look at all, but a true sauntering of the eye.

SEPTEMBER 13, 1856

Ascended the hill. The barberries are abundant there, and already handsomely red—though not much more than half turned. Was surprised at the profusion of autumnal dandelions in their prime on *the top of the hill*— about the oaks. Never saw them thicker in a meadow. A cool spring-suggesting yellow. They reserve their force till this season—though they begin so early. Cool to the eye, as the creak of the cricket to the ear.

SEPTEMBER 13, 1858

Fringed gentian out well—on easternmost edge of the Painted Cup Meadows, by wall.

fringed gentian (*Gentianopsis crinita*)

SEPTEMBER 13, 1859

The *Bidens chrysanthemoides* [large bur-marigold, *B. laevis*], now apparently in its prime by the river, now almost dazzles you with its great sunny disk. I feast my eyes on it annually. It grows but sparingly near the village—but those few never fail to make their appearance at last. The yellow lily's is a cool yellow in comparison but in this is seen the concentrated heat of autumn.

SEPTEMBER 14, 1852

Methinks it is the *Amaranthus hypochondriacus,* prince's feather, with "bright red purple flowers" and sanguine stem on Emerson's muck heap in the Turnpike.

SEPTEMBER 14, 1856

Now for the *Aster Tradescanti* [small white aster, *Symphyotrichum racemosum*] along low roads—like the Turnpike—swarming with butterflies and bees. Some of them are pink. How ever unexpected are these later flowers. You thought that nature had about wound up her affairs. You had seen what she could do this year, and had not noticed a few weeds by the roadside, or mistook them for the remains of summer flowers now hastening to their fall. You thought you knew every twig and leaf by the roadside, and nothing more was to be looked for there—and now to your surprise these ditches are crowded with millions of little stars.

SEPTEMBER 14, 1859

The *Spiranthes cernua* has a sweet scent like the clethra's.

SEPTEMBER 17, 1851

Saw at James Baker's a buttonwood tree with a swarm of bees now three years in it, but honey and all inaccessible.

SEPTEMBER 18, 1859

From the observation of this year I should say that the fringed gentian opened before the witch hazel—for though I know many more localities of the last than the first, I do not find the last out till today, and it cannot have been out but a day or two.

prince's feather (*Amaranthus hypochondriacus*)

SEPTEMBER 19, 1852

The soapwort gentian cheers and surprises—with solid bulbs of blue from the shade—the stale grown purplish. It abounds along the river, after so much has been mown.

SEPTEMBER 19, 1854

Thinking this afternoon of the prospect of my writing lectures and going abroad to read them the next winter, I realized how incomparably great the advantages of obscurity and poverty which I have enjoyed so long (and may still perhaps enjoy). I thought with what more than princely, with what poetical leisure I had spent my years hitherto, without care or engagement, fancy free. I have given myself up to nature. I have lived so many springs and summers and autumns and winters as if I had nothing else to do but *live* them—and imbibe whatever nutriment they had for me. I have spent a couple of years, for instance, with the flowers chiefly, having none other so binding engagement as to observe when they opened. I could have afforded to spend a whole fall observing the changing tints of the foliage.

Am surprised to find the *Polygonum Pennsylvanicum* abundant by the road-side near the bank—first saw it the other day at Brattleboro. This makes, as I reckon, twenty polygonums that I know—all but *cilinode* and *Virginianum* in Concord.

SEPTEMBER 21, 1852

The small skullcap and cress and the mullein still in bloom. I see pigeon woodpeckers oftener now with their light rears. Birches and elms begin to turn yellow—and ferns are quite yellow or brown in many places. I see many tall clustered bluish asters by the brooks like the *A. undulatus* [wavy-leaved aster, *Symphyotrichum undulatum*]. The blue-stemmed goldenrod is abundant, bright and in its prime. . . .

sycamore (buttonwood, *Platanus occidentalis*)

As I was walking through the maple swamp by the Corner Spring I was surprised to see apples on the ground—and at first supposed that some-body had dropped them, but looking up I detected a wild apple tree, as tall and slender as the young maples and not more than five inches in diameter at the ground. This had blossomed and borne fruit this year. The apples were quite mellow and of a very agreeable flavor—though they had a rusty-scraperish look—and I filled my pockets with them. The squirrels had found them out before me. It is an agreeable surprise to find in the midst of a swamp so large and edible a fruit as an apple.

Pennsylvania smartweed (pinkweed, *Persicaria pensylvanica*)

SEPTEMBER 21, 1854

With this bright clear but rather cool air the bright yellow of the autumnal dandelion is in harmony, and the heads of the dilapidated goldenrods. The gentian is already frostbitten almost as soon as it is open. Those pretty little white oak acorn stars of three rays are now quite common on the ground.

SEPTEMBER 21, 1859

The red nesaea blazing along the Assabet above the powder mills.

SEPTEMBER 22, 1851

I am astonished to see how brown and sere the groundsel or "fire weed" on hillside by Heywood's Meadow, which has been touched by frost, already is—as if it had died long months ago, or a fire had run through it. It is a very tender plant.

SEPTEMBER 22, 1852

Sophia has in her herbarium and has found in Concord these which I have not seen this summer.

Pogonia verticillata [whorled pogonia, *Isotria verticillata*], Hubbard's Second Wood. Bigelow says July.

Trillium erythrocarpum [painted trillium, *T. undulatum*], Bigelow says May and June.

Uvularia perfoliata, Bigelow says May.

SEPTEMBER 22, 1859

I see the fall dandelions all closed in *the rain* this afternoon. Do they then open only in fair or cloudy forenoons—and cloudy afternoons?

SEPTEMBER 23, 1852

The sarothra in bloom. The wind from the north has turned the white lily pads wrong side up so that they look red and their stems are slanted upstream. Almost all the yellow ones have disappeared.

SEPTEMBER 23, 1857

I see yellow pinesap, in the woods just east of where the beeches used to stand, just done, but the *red* variety is very common and quite fresh generally there.

whorled pogonia (*Pogonia verticillata=Isotria verticillata*)

Not only foul and poisonous weeds grow in our tracks — but our vileness
and luxuriance make simple and wholesome plants rank and weed-like. . . .
I can detect the site of the shanties that have stood all along the railroads
by the ranker vegetation. I do not go there for delicate wildflowers. . . .

So live that only the most beautiful wildflowers will spring up where
you have dwelt. Harebells, violets, and blue-eyed grass.

SEPTEMBER 23, 1860

Red pinesap by north side of Yew Path some ten rods east of yew — not
long done. The root of the freshest has a *decided* checkerberry scent and for
a long time — a week after — in my chamber the bruised plant has a very
pleasant earthy sweetness.

SEPTEMBER 24, 1851

At Clematis Brook I perceive that the pods or follicles of the *Asclepias
Syriaca* point upward. (Did they before all point down?) They are already

harebell (*Campanula rotundifolia*)

bursting. I release some seeds with the long fine silk attached. The fine threads fly apart, open with a spring as soon as released, and then ray themselves out into a hemispherical form, each thread freeing itself from its neighbor and all reflecting prismatic tints. The seeds besides are winged, I let one go and it rises slowly and uncertainly at first, now driven this way then that, by airs which I cannot perceive, and I fear it will make ship-wreck against the neighboring wood—but no, as it approaches it, it surely rises above it and then feeling the strong north wind it is borne off rapidly in the opposite direction, ever rising higher and higher, and tossing and heaved about with every commotion, till at a hundred feet above the earth and fifty rods off steering south I lose sight of it. How many myriads go sailing away at this season over hill and meadow and river, to plant their race in new localities, on various tacks until the wind lulls, who can tell how many miles. And for this end these silken streamers have been per-fecting all summer, snugly packed in this light chest, a perfect adaptation to this end—a prophecy of the fall and of future springs. Who could be-lieve in prophecies of Daniel or of Miller that the world would end this summer while one milkweed with faith matured its seeds!

SEPTEMBER 24, 1854
Catnip still in bloom.

SEPTEMBER 24, 1859
The poke on Eb. Hubbard's hillside has been considerably frostbitten be-fore the berries are one-third ripe. It is in flower still. Great drooping cylindrical racemes of *blackish* purple berries six inches or more in length, tapering a little toward the end. Great flat blackish and ripe berries at base with green ones and flowers at the other end.

All on brilliant purple or crimson purple peduncle and pedicels. . . .[13]

Am surprised to find, by Botrychium Swamp, a *Rhus radicans* which is quite a tree by itself. It is about nine feet high by nine in width—growing in the midst of a clump of barberry bushes which it overhangs. It is now at the height of its change, very handsome scarlet and yellow, and I did not at first know what it was.

SEPTEMBER 25, 1857
You notice here the dark blue domes of the soapwort gentian in cool and shady places under the bank. . . .

Dogwood (*Rhus venenata*) [poison sumac, *Toxicodendron vernix*] is yet but pale scarlet or yellowish.

Edward Hoar says he found last year *Datura Stramonium* in their garden. Add it then to our plants.

Nabalus albus [white lettuce, *Prenanthes alba*] still common — though much past prime. Though concealed amid trees I find three humblebees on one.

The increasing scarlet and yellow tints around the meadows and the river remind me of the opening of a vast flower bud. They are the petals of its corolla, which is of the width of the valleys. It is the flower of autumn

poison ivy (*Rhus radicans=Toxicodendron radicans*)

whose expanding bud just begins to blush. As yet however in the forest there are very few changes of foliage.

SEPTEMBER 26, 1859
The *Solanum dulcamara* berries are another kind which grows in drooping clusters. I do not know any clusters more graceful and beautiful than these drooping cymes of scarlet or translucent cherry-colored elliptical berries with steel-blue (or lead?) purple pedicels (not peduncles) like those leaves on the tips of the branches. These in the water at the bend of the river are peculiarly handsome, they are so long an oval or ellipse. No berries methinks are so well spaced and agreeably arranged in their drooping cymes—somewhat hexagonally like a honeycomb. Then what a variety of color! The peduncle and its branches are green, the pedicels and sepals only that rare steel-blue purple, and the berries a clear translucent cherry red. They hang more gracefully over the river's brim than any pendants in a lady's ear.

jimsonweed (*Datura stramonium*)

SEPTEMBER 27, 1852

The touch-me-not seed vessels go off like pistols—shoot their seeds off like bullets. They explode in my hat.

The arum berries are now in perfection, cone-shaped spikes an inch and a half long of scarlet or vermilion-colored irregular somewhat pear-shaped berries springing from a purplish core. They are exactly the color of bright sealing wax, or I believe the painted tortoise's shell—on club-shaped peduncles. The changed leaves of this are delicately white especially beneath. Here and there lies prostrate on the damp leaves or ground this conspicuous red spike. The medeola berries are common now and the large red berries of the panicled Solomon's seal.

climbing nightshade (bitter nightshade, *Solanum dulcamara*)

SEPTEMBER 28, 1851

A warm, damp, mistling day—without much wind. The white pines in Hubbard's Grove have now a pretty distinct particolored look—green and yellow mottled—reminding me of some plants like the milkweed expanding with maturity and pushing off their downy seeds. They have a singularly soft look. For a week or ten days I have ceased to look for new flowers or carry my botany in my pocket. The fall dandelion is now very fresh and abundant in its prime. . . .

The swamp contains beautiful specimens of the sidesaddle flower, *Sarracenia purpurea,* better called pitcher plant. They ray out around the dry scape and flower which still remain, resting on rich uneven beds of a coarse reddish moss through which the small-flowered andromeda puts up, presenting altogether a most rich and luxuriant appearance to the eye. Though the moss is comparatively dry, I cannot walk without upsetting the numerous pitchers which are now full of water and so wetting my feet. I once accidentally sat down on such a bed of pitcher plants and found an uncommonly wet seat where I expected a dry one. These leaves are of various colors from plain green to a rich striped yellow or deep red. No plants are more richly painted and streaked than the inside of the broad lips of these.

OCTOBER 2, 1852

How much more beautiful the lakes now like Fair Haven surrounded by the autumn-tinted woods and hills, as in an ornamented frame. Some maples in sproutlands are of a delicate pure clear unspotted red inclining to crimson, surpassing most flowers. I would fain pluck the whole tree and carry it home for a nosegay.

OCTOBER 2, 1856

The scarlet leaves and stem of the rhexia some time out of flower makes almost as bright a patch in the meadow now as the flowers did—with its bristly leaves. Its seed vessels are perfect little cream pitchers of graceful form. The mountain sumac now a dark scarlet quite generally.

OCTOBER 2, 1857

There is a more or less general reddening of the leaves at this season—down to the cinquefoil and mouse-ear, sorrel and strawberry under our feet.

White oaks are still quite green with a few distinct *red* leaves intermixed. A great many red maples are merely yellow—more scarlet in some cases deepening to crimson. . . .

The fringed gentian at Hubbard's Close has been out some time and most of it already withered. In the clintonia swamp I see where some animal has been getting the seeds of the skunk cabbage out of their pericarp.

OCTOBER 3, 1860
The hard frost of September 28, 29, and 30, and especially of October 1st has suddenly killed, crisped, and caused to fall a great many leaves of ash, hickory, etc., etc. . . . Has killed all the burdock flowers and no doubt many others.

burdock (*Arctium minus*)

OCTOBER 5, 1851

Still purplish asters, and late goldenrods, and fragrant life everlasting, and purple gerardia, great bidens, etc., etc. . . . The Norway cinquefoil and a smaller cinquefoil are still in blossom and also the late buttercup. . . . Witch hazel now in bloom. . . . The pale lobelia still blooms freshly. The rough hawkweed holds up its globes of yellowish fuzzy seeds as well as the panicled.

OCTOBER 5, 1858

8 A.M.—I go to Hubbard's Close to see when the fringed gentians open. They *begin* to open *in the sun* about 8:30 A.M., or say 9.

OCTOBER 7, 1857

I go across Bartonia Meadow direct to Bear Garden Hillside. Approaching the sand slide, I see some fifty rods off looking toward the sun the top of the maple swamp just appearing over the sheeny russet edge of the hills—a strip apparently twenty rods long and ten feet deep, of the most intensely brilliant scarlet-orange and yellow, equal to any flowers or fruits or any tints ever painted.

OCTOBER 8, 1852

P.M.—Walden.

Canada snapdragon, a few flowers at top. Everlastings, field trefoil, shepherd's purse, door grass, white goldenrod, fresh tansy, veiny-leaved hawkweed.

OCTOBER 8, 1856

I notice a large toad amid the dead leaves in the woods at *Chimaphila maculata*—colored like the leaves a *much* darker brown than usual, proving that they resemble the ground they occupy.

OCTOBER 9, 1851

The witch hazel here is in full blossom, on this magical hillside [Lee's Cliff], while its broad yellow leaves are falling. Some bushes are completely bare of leaves, and leather-colored they strew the ground. It is an extremely interesting plant—October and November's child—and yet reminds me of the very earliest spring. Its blossoms smell like the spring, like the willow catkins. By their color as well as fragrance they belong to the

saffron dawn of the year. Suggesting amid all these signs of autumn, falling leaves and frost, that the life of nature, by which she eternally flourishes, is untouched. It stands here in the shadow on the side of the hill, while the sunlight from over the top of the hill lights up its topmost sprays and yellow blossoms. Its spray so jointed and angular is not to be mistaken for any other. I lie on my back with joy under its boughs. While its leaves fall, its blossoms spring. The autumn then is indeed a spring. All the year is a spring. I see two blackbirds high overhead going south, but I am going north in my thought with these hazel blossoms.

It is a faery place. This is a part of the immortality of the soul. When I was thinking that it bloomed too late for bees or other insects to extract honey from its flowers, that perchance they yielded no honey, I saw a bee upon it. How important then to the bees this late-blossoming plant!

OCTOBER 9, 1852
Touch-me-not, self-heal, *Bidens cernua,* ladies'-tresses, cerastium, dwarf tree primrose, butter-and-eggs abundant, prenanthes, sium, silvery cinquefoil, mayweed.

witch-hazel (*Hamamelis virginiana*)

The air this morning is full of bluebirds—and again it is spring. There are many things to indicate the renewing of spring at this season. The blossoming of spring flowers—not to mention the witch hazel—the notes of spring birds, the springing of grain and grass and other plants.

spotted wintergreen (*Chimaphila maculata*)

butter-and-eggs (*Linaria vulgaris*)

OCTOBER 10, 1858

I find the fringed gentian abundantly open at 3 and at 4 P.M. (in fact, it must be all the afternoon). Open to catch the cool October sun and air in its low position. Such a dark blue! Surpassing that of the male bluebird's back, who must be encouraged by its presence.

OCTOBER 10, 1860

In August '55, I leveled for the artificial pond at Sleepy Hollow [cemetery]. They dug gradually for three or four years and completed the pond last year in '59. . . . I find today several small patches of the large yellow and the kalmiana lily [small yellow pond-lily, *Nuphar microphylla*] already established. Thus in the midst of death we are in life. . . . You have only to dig a pond anywhere in the fields hereabouts—and you will soon have not only waterfowl, reptiles, and fishes in it, *but* also the usual water plants, as lilies, etc. You will no sooner have got your pond dug than nature will begin to stock it.

OCTOBER 11, 1856

The patches of huckleberries on Conantum are now red. Here on the Cliffs are fresh poke flowers and small snapdragon and corydalis. The white goldenrod is still common here, and covered with bees.

OCTOBER 12, 1851

Yesterday afternoon saw by the brookside above Emerson's the dwarf primrose in blossom, the Norway cinquefoil and fall dandelions which are now drying up. The houstonia, buttercups, small goldenrods, and various asters more or less purplish.

OCTOBER 12, 1857

The fringed gentian by the brook opposite is in its prime, and also along the north edge of the Painted Cup Meadows. The stems of the blue vervain, whose flowers and leaves are withered and brown, are nearly as handsome and clean a purple as those of the poke have been—from top to bottom.

OCTOBER 12, 1858

I land at Pinxter Swamp. The leaves of the azaleas are falling—mostly fallen—and revealing the large blossom buds.

So prepared are they for another year. With man all is uncertainty. He does not confidently look forward to another spring. But examine the root of the savory-leaved aster and you will find the new shoots—fair purple shoots—which are to curve upward and bear the next year's flowers already grown half an inch or more in earth. Nature is confident.

OCTOBER 14, 1852
The woods have lost so many leaves they begin to look bare—maples, poplars, etc., chestnuts. Flowers are fast disappearing. Winter may be anticipated. But few crickets are heard.

OCTOBER 14, 1858
On the top of Ball's Hill, nearly halfway its length, the red pinesap, quite fresh, apparently not long in bloom, the flower recurved. As last year I suspect that this variety is later than the yellowish one—of which I have seen none for a *long time*. The last in E. Hubbard's wood is *all* brown and withered. This is a clear and distinct deep red from the ground upward, all but the edges and tips of the petals, and is very handsome amid the withered lower leaves, as it were the latest flower of the year. The roots have not only a sweet earthy but *decidedly* checkerberry scent. At length this fungus-like plant bursts red-ripe stem and all, from the ground. Its deep redness reminds me of the deeper colors of the western sky after the sun has set—a sort of afterglow in the flowery year. I suspect that it is eminently an autumnal flower.

OCTOBER 15, 1853
Silvery cinquefoil.

OCTOBER 16, 1858
The mikania, goldenrods, and *Andropogon scoparius* have now their November aspect, the former showing their dirty white pappus, the last its white plumose hairs. The year is thus acquiring a grizzly look before the snows of winter.

OCTOBER 16, 1859
A cold, clear, Novemberish day. The wind goes down and we do not sail. The buttonbushes are just bare and the black willows partly so, and the

mikania all fairly gray now. I see the buttonbush balls reflected on each side, and each woolgrass head and recurved withered sedge or rush is also doubled by the reflection. . . .

The frost of the 11th which stiffened the ground made new havoc with vegetation—as I perceive many plants have ceased to bloom no doubt. Many *Diplopappus linariifolius* [stiff aster, *Ionactis linariifolia*] is gone to seed, and yellowish globes. Such are the stages in the year's decline. The flowers are at the mercy of the frosts.

OCTOBER 17, 1850

I observed today (October 17th) the small blueberry bushes by the path side, now blood-red, full of white blossoms as in the spring. The blossoms of spring contrasting strangely with the leaves of autumn. The former seemed to have expanded from sympathy with the maturity of the leaves.

OCTOBER 17, 1855

I see the roots of the great yellow lily lying on the mud where they have made a ditch in John Hosmer's meadow for the sake of the mud, gray-colored when old and dry. Some are three and a half inches in diameter with their great eyes or protuberant shoulders where the leaf stalks stood in quincunx order around them. What rank vigor they suggest—like serpents winding amid the mud of the meadow.

OCTOBER 18, 1857

The fringed gentian closes every night and opens every morning in my pitcher.

OCTOBER 18, 1858

The large sugar maples on the Common are now at the height of their beauty. One, the earliest to change, is partly bare. This turned so early and so deep a scarlet that some thought that it was surely going to die. Also the one at the head of the Turnpike reveals its character now as far as you can see it. Yet about ten days ago all but one of these was quite green—and I thought they would not acquire any bright tints. A delicate but warmer than *golden* yellow is the prevailing color—with scarlet cheeks. They are great regular oval masses of scarlet and yellow. . . .

A village needs these innocent stimulants—of bright and cheery prospect—to keep off melancholy and superstition. Show me two villages, one embowered in trees and blazing with all the glories of October, the other a merely *trivial* and treeless waste, and I shall be sure that in the latter will be found the most desperate and hardest drinkers.

What if we were to take half as much pains in protecting them as we do in setting them out—not stupidly tie our horses to the dahlia stems?

OCTOBER 18, 1860

I see spatterdock pads and pontederia in that little pool at south end of Beck Stow's. How did they get there—there is no stream in this one? Indeed we might as well ask how they got anywhere, for all the pools and fields have been stocked thus—and we are not to suppose as many new creations as pools. . . .

This suggests to inquire how any plant came where it is—how, for instance, the pools which were stocked with lilies before we were born or this town was settled, and ages ago, were so stocked—as well as those which we dug. I think that we are warranted only in supposing that the former was stocked in the same way as the latter, and that there was not a sudden new creation—at least since the first. Yet I have no doubt that peculiarities more or less considerable have thus been gradually produced in the lilies thus planted in various pools—in consequence of their various conditions—though they all came originally from one seed.

We find ourselves in a world that is already planted—but is also still being planted as at first. We say of some plants that they grow in wet places and of others that they grow in desert places. The truth is that their seeds are scattered almost everywhere—but here only do they succeed.

Unless you can show me the pool where the lily was created, I shall believe that the oldest fossil lilies which the geologist has detected (if this is found fossil) originated in that locality in a similar manner to those of Beck Stow's.

We see thus how the fossil lilies which the geologist has detected are dispersed, as well as these which we carry in our hands to church.

The development theory implies a greater vital force in nature—because it is more flexible and accommodating, and equivalent to a sort of constant *new* creation.

OCTOBER 19, 1852

At 5 P.M. I found the fringed gentian now somewhat stale and touched by frost, being in the meadow toward Peter's. . . . At this hour the blossoms are tightly rolled and twisted, and I see that the bees have gnawed round holes in their sides to come at the nectar. They have found them though I had not. . . . An hour ago I doubted if fringed gentians were in Concord now—but having found these they as it were surrender, and I hear of them at the bottom of N. Barrett's orchard toward the river, and by Tuttle's (?). They are now at 8 A.M. opening a little in a pitcher. It is too remarkable a flower not to be sought out and admired each year, however rare.

OCTOBER 19, 1856

The *Asclepias Cornuti* pods are now apparently in the midst of discounting. They point at various angles with the stem like a flourish. The pretty brown fishes have loosened and lifted their scales somewhat, are bristling a little. Or, further advanced, the outer part of the down of the upper seeds is blown loose, while they are still retained by the ends of the middle portion in loops attached to the core. These white tufts, ready to burst and take to flight on the least jar, show afar as big as your fist. There they dangle and flutter till they are quite dry and the wind rises. Others again are open and empty—except of the brown core—and you see what a delicate smooth white (slightly cream-colored) lining this casket has.

OCTOBER 20, 1852

Canada snapdragon, tansy, white goldenrod, blue-stemmed ditto. *Aster undulatus,* autumnal dandelion, tall buttercup, yarrow, mayweed. Picking chestnuts on Pine Hill. . . . The small red Solomon's seal berries spot the ground here and there amid the dry leaves. The witch hazel is bare of all but flowers.

OCTOBER 20, 1857

I see two *Chenopodium album* with stems as bright purple and fair as the poke has been—and the calyx lobes enveloping the seeds the same color.

lamb's quarters (goosefoot, *Chenopodium album*)

OCTOBER 21, 1852

Apparently some flowers yield to the frosts—others linger here and there till the snow buries them. Saw that the side-flowering skullcap was killed by the frost. If they grow in some nook out of the way of frosts they last so much the longer. Methinks the frost puts a period to a large class. The goldenrods being dead are now a dingy white along the brooks (white fuzz, dark brown leaves) together with rusty-fuzzy trumpetweeds and asters in the same condition.

This is a remarkable feature in the landscape now—the abundance of dead weeds. The frosts have done it.

OCTOBER 22, 1851

The fragrant life everlasting is still fresh—and the Canada snapdragon still blooms bluely by the roadside.

OCTOBER 22, 1858

You can still pluck a variegated and handsome nosegay on the top of the Cliff. I see a mullein freshly out, very handsome *Aster undulatus,* and an abundance of the little blue snapdragon, and some *Polygonum Persicaria* [lady's-thumb, *Persicaria maculosa*], etc., etc.

OCTOBER 22, 1859

I am surprised to find in the field behind the top of the Cliffs—a little vetch still perfectly pink and *blooming,* where Wheeler had grain a year or two since, with numerous little plump pods four or five eighths of an inch long and commonly four roundish seeds to each. . . .

A marsh hawk sails over Fair Haven Hill.

In the woodpath below the Cliffs I see perfectly fresh and fair *Viola pedata* flowers as in the spring—though but few together. No flower by its second blooming more perfectly brings back to the spring to us.

OCTOBER 23, 1852

This may be called an Indian summer day. It is quite hazy withal and the mountains invisible. I see a horehound turned lake or steel claret color. The yellow lily pads in Hubbard's ditch are fresh as if recently expanded. There are some white lily pads in river still—but very few indeed of the yellow lily. A pasture thistle on Conantum just budded but flat with the ground. The fields generally wear a russet hue. A striped snake out.

OCTOBER 23, 1853

Everywhere in the fields I see the white hoary (ashy colored) scepters of the gray goldenrod. Others are slightly yellowish still. The yellow is gone out of them as the last flake of sunshine disappears from a field when the clouds are gathering. But though their golden hue is gone their reign is not over. Compact puffed masses of seeds ready to take wing. They will send out their ventures from hour to hour the winter through.

OCTOBER 23, 1858

I notice some late rue turned a very clear light yellow. I see some rose leaves (the early smooth) turned a handsome clear yellow—and some (the *R. Carolina*) equally clear and handsome scarlet, or dark red. This is the rule with it.

OCTOBER 24, 1853

Catnip fresh and green and in bloom. . . . Hedge mustard still fresh and in bloom.

OCTOBER 24, 1858

The brilliant autumnal colors are *red* and *yellow* and the various tints—hues and shades of these. Blue is reserved to be the color of the sky, but yellow and red are the colors of the earth flower. Every fruit on ripening, and just before its fall, acquires a bright tint. So do the leaves—so the sky before the end of the day, and the *year* near its setting. October is the red sunset sky— November the later twilight. Color stands for all ripeness and success. We have dreamed that the hero should carry his *color* aloft as a symbol of the ripeness of his virtue. The noblest feature, the eye, is the fairest colored— the jewel of the body. The warrior's flag is the flower which precedes his fruit. He unfurls his flag to the breeze with such confidence and brag as the flower its petals. Now we shall see what kind of fruit will succeed. . . .

The scarlet oak which was quite green the 12th is now completely scarlet—and apparently has been so a few days. This *alone* of our indigenous deciduous trees (the pitch pine is with it) is now in its glory. . . . Look at one completely changed from green to bright dark scarlet—every leaf, as if it had been dipped into a scarlet dye, between you and the sun. Was not this worth waiting for? Little did you think ten days ago that that cold green tree could assume such color as this.

OCTOBER 25, 1852

Mint is still green and wonderfully recreating to smell. I had put such things behind me. It is hard to remember lilies now.

OCTOBER 25, 1860

The thistles which I now see have their heads recurved—which at least saves their down from so great a soaking. But when I pull out the down, the seed is for the most part left in the receptacle (?) in regular order there like the pricks in a thimble. . . . The perfectly dry and bristly involucre which hedges these round, so repulsive externally, is very neat and attractive within—as smooth and tender toward its charge as it is rough and prickly externally toward the foes that might do it injury. It is a hedge of imbricated thin and narrow leafets of a light brown color, beautifully glossy like silk, a most fit receptacle for the delicate downy parachutes of the seed, a cradle lined with silk or satin.

OCTOBER 27, 1853

I love to be reminded of that universal and eternal spring when the minute crimson-starred female flowers of the hazel are peeping forth on the hill-sides. When nature revives in all her pores.

Some less obvious and commonly unobserved signs of the progress of the seasons interest me most—like the loose dangling catkins of the hop-hornbeam or of the black or yellow birch. I can recall distinctly to my mind the image of these things—and that time in which they flourished is glorious as if it were before the fall of man. I see all nature for the first time under this aspect. These features are particularly prominent. As if the first object I saw on approaching this planet in the spring was the catkins of the hop-hornbeam on the hillsides. As I sailed by I saw the yellowish waving sprays.

OCTOBER 27, 1855

There are *many fringed* gentians, now considerably frostbitten, in what was E. Hosmer's meadow between his dam and the road.

OCTOBER 28, 1859

Goldenrods and asters have been altogether *lingering* some days.

OCTOBER 31, 1850

I thought today that it would be pleasing to study the dead and withered plants, the ghosts of plants which now remain in the fields, for they fill almost as large a space to the eye as the green have done. They live not in memory only, but to the fancy and imagination.

OCTOBER 31, 1853

Tansy lingers still by Hubbard's Bridge. But methinks the flowers are disappearing earlier this season than last.

OCTOBER 31, 1857

If you are afflicted with melancholy at this season—go to the swamp and see the brave spears of skunk cabbage buds already advanced toward a new year. Their gravestones are not bespoken yet. Who shall be sexton to them? Is it the winter of their discontent? Do they seem to have lain down to die, despairing of skunk cabbagedom? "Up and at 'em." "Give it to 'em." "Excelsior." "Put it through." These are their mottoes. Mortal human creatures must take a little respite in this fall of the year—their spirits do flag a little. There is a little questioning of destiny—and thinking to go like cowards to where the "weary shall be at rest." But not so with the skunk cabbage. Its withered leaves fall and are transfixed by a rising bud. Winter and death are ignored—the circle of life is complete. Are these false prophets? Is it a lie or a vain boast underneath the skunk cabbage bud, pushing it upward—and lifting the dead leaves with it? They rest with spears advanced—they rest to shoot!

OCTOBER 31, 1858

As I sit on the Cliff there [Lee's Cliff] the sun is now getting low and the woods in Lincoln south and east of me are lit up by its more level rays—and there is brought out a more brilliant redness in the scarlet oaks scattered so equally over the forest, than you would have believed was in them. Every tree of this species which is visible in these directions—even to the horizon—now stands out distinctly red. Some great ones lift their red backs high above the woods near the Codman place, like huge roses with a myriad fine petals, and some more slender ones in a small grove of white pines on Pine Hill in the east, in the very horizon alternating with the pines on the edge of the grove and shouldering them with their red coats—an intense burning red, which would lose some of its strength methinks with every step you might take toward them—look like soldiers in red amid hunters in green. This time it is *Lincoln* green, too. Until the sun thus lit them up you would not have believed that there were so many redcoats in the forest army. Looking westward their colors are lost in a blaze of light—but in other directions the whole forest is a flower garden, in which these late roses burn, alternating with green, while the so-called "gardeners" working here and there perchance beneath with spade and water pot, see only a few little asters amid withered leaves (for the shade that lurks amid their foliage does not report itself at this distance). . . .

These are my China asters, my late garden flowers. It costs me nothing for a gardener. The falling leaves all over the forest are protecting the roots of my plants. Only look at what is to be seen and you will have garden enough—without deepening the soil of your yard. We have only to elevate our view a little to see the whole forest as a garden.

NOVEMBER 1, 1851

This on my way to Conantum, 2:30 P.M. It is a bright clear warm November day. I feel blessed. I love my life. I warm toward all nature.

The woods are now much more open than when I last observed them. The leaves have fallen and they let in light and I see the sky through them as through a crow's wing in every direction. . . .

Fall dandelions look bright still. The grass has got a new greenness in spots.

At this season there are stranger sparrows or finches about. The skunk cabbage is already pushing up again. The alders have lost their leaves, and the willows except (the last) a few shriveled ones.

NOVEMBER 1, 1858

A man dwells in his native valley like a corolla in its calyx, like an acorn in its cup. *Here,* of course, is all that you love, all that you expect, all that you are.

NOVEMBER 2, 1853

The Canada snapdragon is still fresh and in flower by roadside near pond, and a sprig from root of *Solidago nemoralis.* . . .

I might put by themselves the November flowers—flowers which survive severe frosts and the fall of the leaf. I see hedge mustard very fresh.

NOVEMBER 2, 1858

The large scarlet oak trees and treetops in woods perhaps—especially on hills apparently are late because raised above the influence of the early frosts. Methinks they are as bright even this *dark* day as I ever saw them. The blossoming of the scarlet oak! The forest flower—surpassing all in splendor (at least since the maple). . . . When I rise to a hilltop a thousand of these great oak roses—distributed on every side as far as the horizon. This my unfailing prospect for a fortnight past as surely as I rose to a hilltop. This late forest flower surpasses all that spring or summer could do. Their colors were but rare and dainty specks—which made no impression on a distant eye. Now it is an extended forest or a mountainside that bursts into bloom through or along which we may journey from day to day.

NOVEMBER 4, 1855

The autumnal dandelion sheltered by this apple tree trunk is drooping and half closed and shows but half its yellow this dark late wet day in the fall.

NOVEMBER 4, 1858

If about the last of October you ascend any hill in the outskirts of the town and look over the forest you will see amid the brown of other oaks which are now withered and the green of the pines, the bright red tops or *crescents* of the scarlet oaks very equally and thickly distributed on all sides even to the horizon. Complete trees standing exposed—the edges of the pond—where you have never suspected them, or their tops only in the recesses of the forest surface, or perhaps towering above the surrounding trees, or reflecting a warm rose red from the very edge of the horizon in favorable lights. All this you will see, and much more, if you are prepared to see it—if you *look* for it. Otherwise, regular and universal as this phenomenon is, you will think for threescore years and ten that all the wood is at this season sere and brown. Objects are concealed from our view—not so much because they are out of the course of our visual ray as because there is no intention of the mind and eye toward them. We do not realize how far and widely—or how near and narrowly we are to look. The greater part of the phenomena of nature are for this reason concealed to us all our lives. Here too, as in political economy, the supply answers to the demand. Nature does not cast pearls before swine. There is just as much beauty visible to us in the landscape as we are prepared to appreciate—not a grain more. The actual objects which one person will see from a particular hilltop are just as different from those which another will see as the persons are different. The scarlet oak must in a sense be in your eye when you go forth. We cannot see anything—until we are possessed with the idea of it, and then we can hardly see anything else. In my botanical rambles I find that first the idea or image of a plant occupies my thoughts though it may at first seem very foreign to this locality—and for some weeks or months I go thinking of it and expecting it unconsciously, and at length I surely *see* it, and it is henceforth an actual neighbor of mine. This is the history of my finding a score or more of some plants which I could name.

NOVEMBER 5, 1855

I see the shepherd's purse, hedge mustard, and red clover—November flowers.

NOVEMBER 6, 1853

Still the Canada snapdragon, yarrow, autumnal dandelion, tansy, shepherd's purse, silver cinquefoil, witch hazel. The sweet briar hips are abundant and fresh, a dozen sometimes crowded in a space of two inches square.

NOVEMBER 8, 1850

Dry goldenrods now turned gray and white lint our clothes as we walk. And the drooping downy seed vessels of the epilobium remind us of the summer. Perchance you will meet with a few solitary asters in the dry fields with a little color left. The sumac is stripped of everything but its cone of red berries.

NOVEMBER 11, 1850

Now is the time for wild apples. I pluck them as a wild fruit native to this quarter of the earth—fruit of old trees that have been dying ever since I was a boy and are not yet dead. From the appearance of the tree you would expect nothing but lichens to drop from it—but underneath your faith is rewarded by finding the ground strewn with spirited fruit.

NOVEMBER 12, 1853
Tansy is very fresh still in some places.

NOVEMBER 14, 1852
Still yarrow, tall buttercup, and tansy.

NOVEMBER 14, 1853
Mallows still in bloom, and hedge mustard.

NOVEMBER 15, 1857
The water is frozen solid in the leaves of the pitcher plants.

common yarrow (*Achillea millefolium*)

There seems to be in the fall a sort of attempt at a spring, a rejuvenescence as if the winter were not expected by a part of nature. Violets, dandelions, and some other flowers blossom again, and mulleins and innumerable other plants begin again to spring and are only checked by the increasing cold. There is a slight uncertainty whether there will be any winter this year. . . .

My Journal should be the record of my love. I would write in it only of the things I love. My affection for any aspect of the world. What I love to think of. I have no more distinctness or pointedness in my yearnings than an expanding bud, which does indeed point to flower and fruit, to summer and autumn, but is aware of the warm sun and spring influence only. I feel ripe for something yet do nothing, can't discover what that thing is. I feel fertile merely. It is seed time with me. I have lain fallow long enough.

common mallow (*Malva neglecta*)

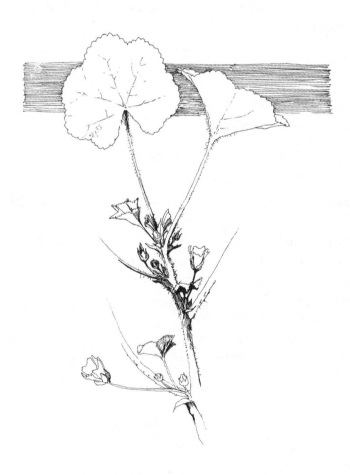

NOVEMBER 18, 1852

Yarrow and tansy still. These are cold gray days.

NOVEMBER 19, 1850

If you penetrate to some warm recess under a cliff in the woods you will
be astonished at the amount of summer life that still flourishes there. No
doubt more of the summer's life than we are aware of thus slips by and
outmaneuvers the winter—gliding from fence to fence. I have no doubt
that a diligent search in proper places would discover many more of our
summer flowers thus lingering till the snow came, than we suspect. It is as
if the plant made no preparation for winter.

NOVEMBER 20, 1857

If a man is rich and strong anywhere it must be in his native soil. Here
I have been these forty years learning the language of these fields that I
may the better express myself. If I should travel to the prairies, I should
much less understand them, and my past life would serve me but ill to
describe them.

Many a weed here stands for more of life to me than the big trees of
California would if I should go there.

NOVEMBER 24, 1850

Plucked a buttercup on Bear Hill today.

NOVEMBER 24, 1851

Setting stakes in the swamp (Ministerial). Saw seven black ducks fly out
of the peat hole. Saw there also a tortoise still stirring. The painted tortoise I believe.

Found on the south side of the swamp the *Lygodium palmatum* which
Bigelow calls the only climbing fern in our latitude—an evergreen called
with others snake tongue, as I find in Loudon.

NOVEMBER 30, 1851

The *Lygodium palmatum* is quite abundant on that side of the swamp—
twining round the goldenrods, etc., etc.

DECEMBER I, 1856

The bluecurls' chalices stand empty—and waiting evidently to be filled with ice.

DECEMBER 6, 1859

Came upon a round bed of tansy, half a dozen feet in diameter, which was withered quite *black,* as seen above the snow—blacker than any plant I remember.

DECEMBER 7, 1852

Perhaps the warmest day yet. True Indian summer. The walker perspires. The shepherd's purse is in full bloom, the andromeda not turned red.

DECEMBER 8, 1854

Winter has come unnoticed by me, I have been so busy writing. This is the life most lead in respect to nature. How different from my habitual one! It is hasty coarse and trivial as if you were a spindle in a factory. The other is leisurely fine and glorious, like a flower.

DECEMBER 9, 1859

How prominent the *late* or fall flowers are, now withered above the snow— the goldenrods and asters, Roman wormwood, etc., etc. These late ones have a sort of life extended into winter, hung with icy jewelry.

DECEMBER 10, 1856

It is remarkable how suggestive the slightest drawing as a memento of things seen. For a few years past I have been accustomed to make a rude sketch in my journal of plants, ice, and various natural phenomena—and though the fullest accompanying description may fail to recall my experience, these rude outline drawings do not fail to carry me back to that time and scene. It is as if I saw the same thing again. And I may again attempt to describe it in words if I choose.

DECEMBER 14, 1851

The now dry and empty but clean-washed cups of the bluecurls spot the half snow-covered grainfields. Where lately was a delicate blue flower now all the winter are held up these dry chalices. What mementos to stand above the snow!

DECEMBER 19, 1850

I see where the snow birds have picked the seeds of the Roman worm-wood and other weeds and have covered the snow with the shells and husks. The smilax berries are as plump as ever. The catkins of the alders are as tender and fresh-looking as ripe mulberries. The dried chokecherries so abundant in the swamp are now quite sweet. The witch hazel is covered with fruit and droops over gracefully like a willow, the yellow foundation of its flowers still remaining. I find the sweet gale, *Myrica,* by the river also. The wild apples are frozen as hard as stones and rattle in my pockets but I find that they soon thaw when I get to my chamber and yield a sweet cider. I am astonished that the animals make no more use of them.

DECEMBER 23, 1859

The now bare or empty heads of the liatris look somewhat like dusky daisies surmounted by a little button instead of a disk. The last—a stiff round parchment-like skin, the base on which its flowerets stood—is pierced by many little round holes just like the end of a thimble, where the cavities are worn through, and it is convex like that. It readily scales off and you can look through it.

DECEMBER 25, 1856

At Lee's Cliff I pushed aside the snow with my foot and got some fresh green catnip for Min.

DECEMBER 26, 1855

Here are asters, savory-leaved, whose flat imbricated calyxes three quar-ters of an inch over are surmounted and inclosed in a perfectly transpar-ent ice button like a glass knob—through which you see the reflections of the brown calyx. These are very common. Each little blue-curls calyx has a spherical button like those brass ones on little boys' jackets—little sprigs on them—and the pennyroyal has still smaller spheres more regularly arranged around the stem, chandelier-wise, and still smells through the ice.

JANUARY 1, 1853

Some weeds bear the ice in masses—some like the trumpetweed and tansy in balls for each dried flower. What a crash of jewels as you walk. The most careless walker who never deigned to look at these humble weeds before cannot help observing them now. This is why the herbage is left to stand dry in the fields all winter.

JANUARY 5, 1851

The catkins of the alders are now frozen stiff!!

JANUARY 9, 1853

Pulling up the johnswort on the face of the Cliff I am surprised to see the signs of unceasing growth about the roots—fresh shoots two inches long, white with red leafets, and all the radical part quite green. The leaves of the crowfoot also are quite green and carry me forward to spring. I dig one up with a stick, and pulling it to pieces I find deep in the center of the plant just beneath the ground, surrounded by all the tender leaves that are to precede it, the blossom bud about half as big as the head of a pin, perfectly white. (I open one next day, and it is yellow.) There it patiently sits or slumbers, how full of faith, informed of a spring which the world has never seen, the promise and prophecy of it shaped somewhat like some Eastern temples, in which a bud-shaped dome o'ertops the whole.

JANUARY 10, 1856

We are reduced to admire buds even like the partridges—and bark like the rabbits and mice. The great yellow and red forward-looking buds of the azalea, the plump red ones of the blueberry, and the fine sharp red ones of the panicled andromeda, sleeping along its stem. The speckled black alder, the rapid-growing dogwood, the pale brown and cracked blueberry, etc. Even a little shining bud which lies sleeping behind its twig and dreaming of spring, perhaps half concealed by ice, is object enough.

JANUARY 10, 1858

The north side of Walden is a warm walk in sunny weather. If you are sick and despairing, go forth in winter and see the red alder catkins dangling at the extremities of the twigs, all in the wintry air—like long hard mulberries, promising a new spring and the fulfillment of all our hopes. We prize any tenderness, any softening in the winter—catkins, birds' nests, insect life, etc., etc.

The most I got perchance is the sight of a mulberry-like red catkin which I know has a dormant life in it, seemingly greater than my own.

JANUARY 11, 1854

The humblest weed is indescribably beautiful—of purest white and richest form. The hogweed [common ragweed] becomes a fairy's wand. The blue-curls rising from bare gray sand is perhaps particularly beautiful. . . . It is an exquisitely delicate frost plant trembling like swan's down.

JANUARY 28, 1852

About Brister's Spring the ferns which have been covered with snow and the grass are still quite green. The skunk cabbage in the water is already pushed up and I find the pinkish head of flowers within its spathe bigger than a pea.

JANUARY 31, 1854

If you would know what are my winter thoughts look for them in the partridge's crop. They are like the laurel buds—some leaf, some blossom buds—which though food for such indigenous creatures will not expand into leaves and flowers until summer comes.

FEBRUARY 4, 1858

Discover the *Ledum latifolium* quite abundant over a space about six rods in diameter just east of the small pond hole [Charles Smith Swamp]—growing with the *Andromeda calyculata, [A.] Polifolia, Kalmia glauca*, etc. . . .

The ledum bears a *general* resemblance to the water andromeda, with its dark reddish purplish or rather mulberry leaves—reflexed—but nearer it is distinguished by its coarseness, the perfect tent form of its upper leaves, and the *large* conspicuous terminal roundish (strictly oval) red buds, nearly as big as the swamp pink's but rounded. The woolly stem for a couple of inches beneath the bud is frequently bare and conspicuously club-shaped. The rust on the undersides of the leaves seems of a lighter color than that of Maine. The seed vessels (which open at the base *first*) still hold on. This plant might easily be confounded with the water andromeda—by a care-

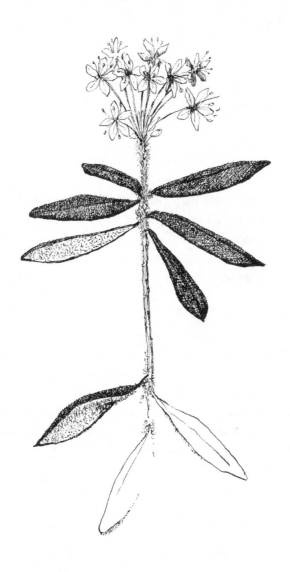

Labrador tea (*Ledum latifolium=Rhododendron groenlandicum*)

less observer. When I showed it to a teamster, he was *sure that he had seen* it often in the woods, but the sight of the woolly underside staggered him. . . . As usual with the finding of new plants—I had presentiment that I should find the ledum in Concord. It is a remarkable fact that, in the case of the most interesting plants which I have discovered in this vicinity, I have anticipated finding them perhaps a year before the discovery.

FEBRUARY 5, 1852

I suspect that the child plucks its first flower with an insight into its beauty and significance which the subsequent botanist never retains.

FEBRUARY 6, 1852

I asked a learned and accurate naturalist who is at the same time the courteous guardian of a public library to direct me to those works which contained the more particular *popular* account or *biography* of particular flowers from which the botanies I had met with appeared to draw sparingly—for I trusted that each flower had had many lovers and faithful describers in past times—but he informed me that I had read all, that no one was acquainted with them, they were only catalogued like his books.

FEBRUARY 26, 1854

The weeds, trees, etc., are covered with a glaze. The bluecurl cups are overflowing with icy drops.

FEBRUARY 28, 1857

At the Cliff, the tower mustard, early crowfoot, and perhaps buttercup appear to have started of late. It takes several years' faithful search to learn where to look for the earliest flowers.

Notes

1. Silver maple, *Acer saccharinum.* See Angelo, "Thoreau as Botanist."

2. A triangular plot of land, called a "heater piece" because it resembled a triangular clothes iron.

3. Poison ivy, *Rhus radicans.* See Angelo, "Thoreau as Botanist."

4. Only the black spruce, *Picea mariana,* occurred in Concord. See Angelo, "Thoreau as Botanist."

5. In his 1902 article "Thoreau and the Pines," James B. Wood wrote, "Thoreau once asked me if I knew that a white pine tree had a beautiful blossom on its very top. I told him I had never seen one. He said that once in June, he had climbed to the top of a pine tree and found the blossom, but he had never found any person who had ever seen one."

6. A pencilled interrogation-point in parenthesis follows here. *Torrey and Allen.*

7. On July 9, 1851, Thoreau wrote, "When I got out of the cars at Porter's, Cambridge, this morning, I was pleased to see the handsome blue flowers of the succory or endive (*Cichorium Intybus*), which reminded me that within the hour I had been whirled into a new botanical region. They must be extremely rare, if they occur at all, in Concord. This weed is handsomer than most garden flowers."

8. In his 1893 "Reminiscences of Thoreau," Horace R. Hosmer wrote that Thoreau found the climbing fern near the Ministerial Swamp. "I never saw such a pleased, happy look on his face as he had that day. He took off his hat, in the crown of which the fern was coiled up, and showed me the dainty, graceful glory of the swamp. He said it had never been seen before in the New England states."

9. Thoreau does not describe the blossom of the groundnut in the Journal, but in *Walden* he writes, "Digging one day for fishworms I discovered the ground-nut (*Apios tuberosa*) on its string, the potato of the aborigines, a sort of fabulous fruit, which I had begun to doubt if I had ever dug and eaten in childhood, as I had told, and had not dreamed it. I had often since seen its crimpled red velvety blossom supported by the stems of other plants without knowing it to be the same."

10. Perhaps not. Ray Angelo identifies the "linear-leafed gerardia" of July 31, 1853, as the same species.

11. According to Ray Angelo, actually creeping spearwort, *Ranunculus reptans.*

12. Thoreau noted the false Solomon's seal on June 18, 1857, near the Highland Light on Cape Cod, writing, "The *Smilacina racemosa* was *just* out of bloom on the bank. They call it the 'wood lily' there. Uncle Sam called it 'snake-corn,' and said it looked like corn when it first came up."

13. The word "poke" appears here, drawn across the page in large characters now (1906) of a dirty light-brown color. The stain is doubtless what remains of the poke berry's purple juice. *Torrey and Allen.*

Botanical Terms

A ROD, which Thoreau frequently used as a unit of measurement, is sixteen and a half feet long. Some botanical terms may also need definition:

ACHENE: a dry, one-seeded fruit that does not separate or split open when mature

AMENT: see *catkin*

ANTHER: the pollen-bearing part of the stamen

APETALOUS: without petals

APPRESSED: lying close and flat and pointing toward the apex of a plant, usually referring to leaves growing up against the stem

AWN: a fine, bristlelike appendage

AXIL: the juncture where a lateral organ, such as a leaf, joins a main axis, such as a stem

BRACT: a specialized leaf or leaflike part, usually at the base of a flower or inflorescence

CALYX: the sepals or outermost group of floral parts

CATKIN: a slender, usually dangling inflorescence, with crowded male or female flowers

CILIA: hairs along the margins of a plant's organ

CONNATE: fused to another organ of the same kind, such as flower petals fused to form the tube of a corolla

CONVOLUTE: when each floral organ in a bud overlaps the next, or when one leaf is rolled up inside another leaf

COROLLA: the second (inner) whorl of floral organs, enclosed by the calyx, often consisting of petals

CORYMB: a flat-topped or convex inflorescence in which the outermost flowers are the first to open

CRENATE: with blunt or rounded teeth, scalloped

CULM: the usually jointed and hollow stem of a grass

CYME: a flat-topped or convex cluster of flowers in which the central flower is the first to open

DISSECTED: deeply divided

EFFETE: no longer fertile

FASCICULATED: with leaflets or needles in a bundle or compact cluster

FILIFORM: threadlike

FLORET: an individual true flower contained within an inflorescence

FOLLICLE: a dry, single-chambered fruit that splits along one seam to release its seeds, as in larkspur and milkweed

GLOBOSE: shaped like a sphere

GLUMES: the bracts, usually in pairs, at the base of a grass or sedge spikelet

IMBRICATED: overlapping like shingles on a roof

INFLORESCENCE: the flowering part of a plant, most often applied to a cluster of flowers

INVOLUCRE: a structure that surrounds or supports another, usually a head of flowers

LANCEOLATE: narrowly ovate, broadest in the lower half and tapering to the tip like a spearhead

LEAFET: a little leaf (archaic)

LEAFLETS: the ultimate segments of a compound leaf

NECTARY: a specialized gland that secretes nectar

NUTLET: a small nut

OBLANCEOLATE: lanceolate but broadest in its upper third

OSIER: twig from a willow of the kind used for wickerwork

OVATE: egg-shaped, wider than lanceolate, widest below the middle

PANICLE: a compound raceme, or any loose, diversely branching flower cluster

PEDICEL: a small stalk to a single flower in an inflorescence

PEDUNCLE: the main stalk that supports an inflorescence

PERFOLIATE: wrapped around the stem so that the stem appears to pass through it, as with certain leaves and bracts

PERICARP: the walls of a ripened ovary or fruit

PETIOLE: the stalk of a leaf

PINNATE: a compound leaf with leaflets arranged on each side of a common petiole or axis

PINNATIFID: pinnately cleft, with clefts reaching halfway or more to the midrib

PISTIL: the seed-bearing female organ of a flower, consisting of an ovary, style, and stigma

PLUMOSE: featherlike, with fine hairs branching from an axis

POMACE: the pulpy residue from apples or similar fruit after crushing and pressing

RACEME: a simple, indeterminate inflorescence in which the flowers are carried on short pedicels lying along a common axis, as in the lily of the valley

RACHIS: the central axis of a leaf

RADICAL: springing from the root, or clustered at the base of the stem

RECURVED: bent or curved backwards or downwards

REFLEXED: bent sharply back or down

RETICULATED: net-veined or with ribs that interconnect in a honeycomb pattern

REVOLUTE: rolled under (downward or backward)

SCAPE: the stalk of a flower or inflorescence that rises without leaves from ground level

SEPAL: one of the parts forming the calyx of a flower, usually green

SERRATE: with forward-pointing sharp teeth

SESSILE: without a stalk

SINUS: a notch or depression between two lobes or teeth

SPADIX: an unbranched, fleshy spike with flowers partially embedded in it

SPATHE: a large bract forming a sheath around a spadix

SPIKELET: in grasses and sedges, the structure containing bracts and a number of florets

STAMEN: the male organ of a flower, usually consisting of a filament and an anther

STAMINATE: with stamens

STIGMA: the pollen-receptive end of a pistil, usually sticky

STYLE: the slender part of a pistil, extending from the ovary to the stigma and containing the pollen tube

TERETE: cylindrical or slightly tapering

TERNATE: arranged in a whorl of three

UMBEL: a convex, rounded, or flat-topped inflorescence in which the individual flower stalks rise from about the same point, as in Queen Anne's lace, milkweed, or wild onion

VALVE: the part of an organ that fragments or splits open, such as the toothlike parts of a capsule or pod that splits open when ripe

Key to Place-Names

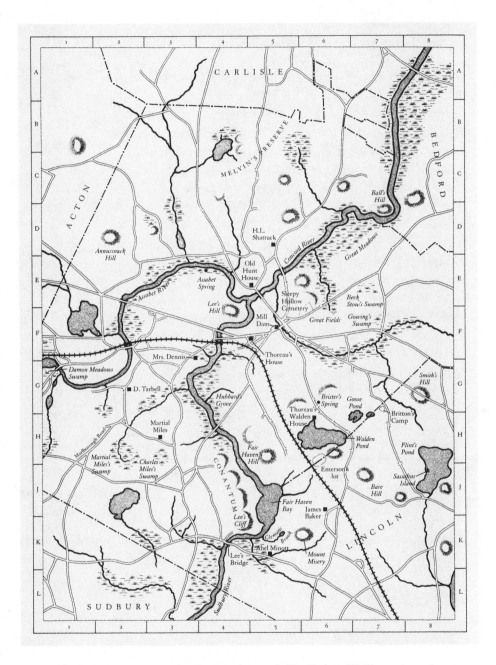

Concord, Massachusetts, based on a map compiled by Herbert W. Gleason in 1906.
(From *Faith in a Seed,* by Henry D. Thoreau. Copyright © 1993 by Island Press.
Reproduced by permission of Island Press, Washington, DC.)

Bibliography

Ahmadjian, Vernon. *Flowering Plants of Massachusetts.* Amherst: University of Massachusetts Press, 1979.

Anderson, Charles R. *Thoreau's World: Miniatures from His Journal.* Englewood Cliffs, NJ: Prentice-Hall, 1971.

Angelo, Ray. *Botanical Index to the Journal of Henry David Thoreau.* Salt Lake City: Gibbs Smith, 1984. Online at www.ray-a.com/ThoreauBotIdx/.

———. "Review of Claims of Species Loss in the Flora of Concord, Massachusetts, Attributed to Climate Change." *Phytoneuron* 2014–84: 1–48. Online at http://phytoneuron.net/2014Phytoneuron/84PhytoN-ConcordMissingSpecies.pdf.

———. *Vascular Flora of Concord, Massachusetts.* Latest revision October 2014. Online at www.ray-a.com/ConcordMassFlora.pdf.

Bosco, Ronald A., editor. *Nature's Panorama: Thoreau on the Seasons.* Amherst: University of Massachusetts Press, 2005.

Case, Kristen, editor. *Thoreau's Kalendar: A Digital Archive of the Phenological Manuscripts of Henry David Thoreau.* University of Maine at Farmington. Online at http://thoreauscalendar.umf.maine.edu/about.html.

Dean, Bradley, ed. *Faith in a Seed: The Dispersion of Seeds and Other Late Natural History Writings by Henry D. Thoreau.* Washington, DC: Island Press, 1993.

———. *Wild Fruits: Thoreau's Rediscovered Last Manuscript.* New York: W. W. Norton, 1999.

Donahue, Brian. *The Great Meadow: Farmers and the Land in Colonial Concord.* New Haven: Yale University Press, 2004.

Eaton, Richard Jefferson. *A Flora of Concord.* Cambridge, MA: Harvard University Museum of Comparative Zoology, 1974.

Foster, David R. *Thoreau's Country: Journey through a Transformed Landscape.* Cambridge, MA: Harvard University Press, 1999.

Gleason, Herbert W. *Thoreau Country.* San Francisco: Sierra Club Books, 1975.

Grant, Steve, editor. *Daily Observations: Thoreau on the Days of the Year.* Amherst: University of Massachusetts Press, 2005.

Grossman, Richard, editor. *A Year with Emerson.* Boston: David R. Godine, 2003.

Harding, Walter, editor. *In the Woods and Fields of Concord*. Salt Lake City: Gibbs Smith, 1982.

———. *Thoreau as Seen by His Contemporaries*. New York: Dover, 1989.

Harding, Walter, and Michael Meyer. *The New Thoreau Handbook*. New York: New York University Press, 1980.

Howarth, William. *The Book of Concord: Thoreau's Life as a Writer*. New York: Penguin, 1983.

Loewer, Peter. *Thoreau's Garden: Native Plants for the American Landscape*. Mechanicsburg, PA: Stackpole Books, 2002.

Maynard, W. Barksdale. *Walden Pond: A History*. New York: Oxford University Press, 2004.

McGregor, Robert Kuhn. *A Wider View of the Universe: Henry Thoreau's Study of Nature*. Urbana, IL: University of Illinois Press, 1997.

Miller, Perry. *Consciousness in Concord: The Text of Thoreau's Hitherto Lost Journal (1840–1841) Together with Notes and a Commentary*. Boston: Houghton Mifflin, 1958.

Primack, Richard B. *Walden Warming: Climate Change Comes to Thoreau's Woods*. Chicago: University of Chicago Press, 2014.

Richardson, Robert D., Jr. *Henry Thoreau: A Life of the Mind*. Oakland: University of California Press, 1986.

Rothwell, Robert L., editor. *Henry David Thoreau: An American Landscape*. New York: Marlowe, 1991.

Thoreau, Henry David. *The Journal of Henry D. Thoreau*. Edited by Bradford Torrey and Francis H. Allen. 1906; reprint ed., New York: Dover, 1962.

———. *Of Woodland Pools, Spring-Holes and Ditches*. Berkeley, CA: Counterpoint, 2010.

———. *The Writings of Henry D. Thoreau*, Online Journal Transcripts, Volumes 18–33. Santa Barbara, CA: University of Santa Barbara. Online at http://thoreau.library.ucsb.edu/writings_journals.html.

———. *The Writings of Henry David Thoreau: Journal, Volumes 1–8*, various editors. Princeton, NJ: Princeton University Press, 1981–2002.

Zwinger, Ann, and Edwin Way Teale. *A Conscious Stillness: Two Naturalists on Thoreau's Rivers*. Amherst: University of Massachusetts Press, 1984.

Index

Page numbers in italics indicate illustrations.

273